D0916818

BLACK BEAR
Seasons in the Wild

TOM ANDERSON

FOREWORD BY WAYNE McCRORY

PHOTOGRAPHS BY
Tom Anderson   Jeanne Drake   Michael H. Francis
Bill Ivy   Wayne Lankinen   Bill S. Lea
Tom & Pat Leeson   McCrory Wildlife Services   Rick McIntyre
John & Ann Mahan   Allan Morgan
James H. Robinson   Tom Walker
Art Wolfe   George Wuernther
Minnesota Department of Natural Resources

VOYAGEUR PRESS

Edited by Helene Jones and Kathy Mallien

94 95 96 5 4 3 2

Library of Congress Cataloging-in-Publication Data

Anderson, Tom, 1951-
    Black bear : seasons in the wild / Tom Anderson.
        p. cm.
    Includes bibliographical references and index.
    ISBN 0-89658-173-X
    ISBN 0-89658-203-5 (pbk.)
    1. Black bear. I. Title.
QL737.C27A53 1992
599.74'446-dc20   91-41365
                                                              CIP

Published by
VOYAGEUR PRESS, INC.
P.O. Box 338, 123 North Second Street
Stillwater, MN 55082 U.S.A.
From Minnesota and Canada 612-430-2210
Toll-free 800-888-9653

Distributed in Canada by
RAINCOAST BOOKS
112 East 3rd Avenue
Vancouver, B.C. V5T 1C8

Voyageur Press books are also available at discounts for quantities for educational, fundraising, premium, or sales-promotion use. For details contact the marketing department.

Front cover, photo copyright by Bill Lea. Page 1, photo copyright by James H. Robinson. Back cover, photo copyright by Jeanne Drake.

To Britta and Maren

AUTHOR'S NOTE
It was a joy to work on this book because I learned so much. Because I am not a bear biologist, I had to go to those who are the experts in their field: Wayne McCrory, Karen Noyce, Craig McLaughlin, Dave Garshelis, Lynn Rogers, Pam Coy, Gary Alt, Chris Servheen, and Stephen Herrero. I owe gratitude to some because they shared through their published work and some because of their invaluable review of the manuscript.

Thanks to my friends and family for putting up with my term of bear craze and for giving me the time I needed to see the book through to its completion.

I would also like to thank the photographers who contributed to the portrayal of the black bear in such a fine manner. Editors Helene Jones and Kathy Mallien deserve a medal for their patience with this project. And I cannot forget to thank friends who offered their support and who kept their eyes peeled for bear literature.

CONTENTS

FOREWORD

Having been raised in a remote, wilderness valley in British Columbia, about three hundred miles north of Spokane, Washington, I learned at an early age what black and grizzly bears were all about. My tutorship and indoctrination into survival in the world of wild bears came about somewhat inadvertently through my father who, as an incurable prospector, often took me on forays after lost silver mines that always seemed to lie at the head of a remote valley in some of the most junglelike avalanche chutes and black and grizzly bear habitats in existence.

Some of my early lessons did not come easy. For example: One day, a large brown-phased black bear ambled up the trail toward us, calmly ignoring my father's frantic banging of pots and pans; the pealing pans, he had reassured me, were nearly as foolproof as the deafening clangs of the cowbell he had forgotten at home. My father didn't believe in carrying a rifle, and my eight-year-old mind was quickly beginning to doubt his wisdom. As the bear sauntered closer, and the pot-banging achieved a frenzied crescendo, my feelings of smallness and vulnerability increased to the point where I hoped that, when the bear took me for supper, it would be done more quickly than the way my cat took mice. At about ten feet, the bear stopped and calmly appraised us. From behind my father's legs (which, like mine, were shaking), I saw that it had one tattered, flopped-over ear and several old scars on its face. Much to my surprise, its teeth weren't bared, and its ancient-looking, small eyes did not stare at me menacingly. In fact, the bear looked quite mellow. Suddenly, it gave a chuff and walked into the undergrowth. My father said it was a big dominant bear that had been merely curious and would probably have been happier if we, instead of it, had moved aside and let the other pass. Perhaps he was right. Little did I know at the time how this brief, but powerful, close contact with a bear would help instill in my psyche a deep respect and downright affection for these shaggy beasts, and how it would lead me into a lifelong career as a wildlife biologist studying and working to save bears in many key areas in western Canada.

And little did I realize then that eventually, on one of the

Left: Photo copyright by Tom & Pat Leeson. Overleaf: Princess Royal Island, British Columbia. Photo copyright by McCrory Wildlife Services.

most memorable of bear days, I would observe a rare, unstudied subspecies of black bear called *Ursus americanus kermodei*. My co-worker, Erica Mallam, my colleagues, and I were roaming a still-unpillaged, misty British Columbia coastal island, where we would conduct conservation research, when we encountered one of the all-white individuals. Years before, I had never imagined that such a form of black bear even existed, let alone that I would witness one in the wilds.

On this particular day, a huge, golden-tinted white Kermode bear suddenly emerged into our field of vision from the thin shrouds of mist that hovered over a stream teeming with spawning salmon. For several spellbound minutes, we watched the bear pad silently along the edge of the wall of towering Sitka spruce trees that lined the creek. The Kermode seemed to float surrealistically in the mist before being swallowed in a wink by the dark, moss-laden rainforest. Suddenly I knew why some people call them the "ghost" or "spirit" bears.

Although the bear did not emerge again, its brief appearance coalesced our selection of remote Princess Royal Island for future studies with a long-thought-out proposal for the setting aside of the entire southern half of the island as one of North America's first black bear sanctuaries. Coincidentally, the white bears in this area had long been revered by Northwest Coast Indians. One legend tells of Raven the Creator, who, wishing to leave a reminder of the last Ice Age, went among the black and brown bears and made every tenth one white.

Given the unprecedented degree of massive clear-cut logging of temperate rainforests on the north end of Princess Royal Island and elsewhere in the range of the Kermodes, combined with increasing threats of poaching, the chances of these bears surviving over the next century are slight. For they, along with the many other varieties of black bear in America, are perhaps one of the most maligned of wildlife species. Conditioning to human foods at garbage dumps and homesteads, rampant clear-cut logging including destruction of old trees used for winter dens, increased poaching combined with excessive hunting and control kills, range fragmentation, habitat loss: All of these factors are slowly but inexorably pushing black bears into decline and local extinction.

But it is not too late, and much needs to and can be done so that humankind and the black bear can live more harmoniously on this planet. Tom Anderson's *Black Bear: Seasons in the Wild* not only tells us eloquently about the wild and beautiful nature of the black bear, but also how, with all our efforts, we can work to ensure its survival.

Wayne McCrory, Wildlife Biologist,
New Denver, British Columbia

INTRODUCTION

Bear. Consider that word for a moment. It carries a mystique not unlike the powers packed in the words *snake, spider, skunk,* and *shark.* These words can be great motivators; for many people, they denote something to be avoided—and the quicker the better.

Time and time again, the bear is painted both artistically and in our minds as a threatening monster, one of the "sinister forces of nature" that stands in the way of our lifestyle. Popular culture and everyday life sketch the picture of this "threat": If there is one line that most of us remember from *The Wizard of Oz,* it is when a wide-eyed Dorothy declares, "Lions and tigers and bears! Oh my!" And does this warning sound familiar, "Watch out, the boss is a bear today"?

As a naturalist-teacher at the Lee and Rose Warner Nature Center, thirty miles northeast of the Twin Cities in Minnesota and just south of the state's prime black bear range, I am often asked by urban schoolchildren if any bears live in the surrounding woods. My answer surprises them: "I doubt it, but it would be great if there were some around here." During my musings on the kids' reactions, I've found the word *bear* elicits contradictory responses. To a young child, *bear* symbolizes comfort, a friend to cuddle up next to at bedtime. As the years of innocence pass by, *bear* becomes more threatening. The animal becomes viewed as being capable of eating not only our cooler-stored food but also our very flesh. These schoolchildren are products of their environment, and for most of them, their world has taught them to fear creatures such as bears.

The reaction to *bear* is a paradox. People have a strange aversion to and love affair with this creature. Folks will lie awake all night in a flimsy tent if they hear any suspicious noise in the dark. In their minds, a troublesome bear lurks. Then the next day, those same folks might drive miles out of their way to view bears from the sanctuary of a car as the beasts scavenge through trash at an open dump.

During the summer and fall, black bears rarely pass up a chance to feed. Similar to its cousin the Alaskan brown bear, the black will take to the rivers to fetch a pink salmon if the opportunity presents itself. (Photo copyright by Tom & Pat Leeson)

By nature, humans are suspicious creatures. We become apprehensive of those things that we don't know much about. If I hear a noise in the dark, my imagination races as it draws pictures of a skulking prowler, a wolf, or perhaps even a bear. A well-directed flashlight might prove the noisemaker to be a nervous cottontail rabbit. Immediately, my heart rate returns to a more normal tempo, and my fears retreat. To overcome some of our fears, we need to erase our ignorance about the object of fright. If I were to be squeamish about snakes, it might be to my advantage to learn about snakes and the role they play in the natural world. The purpose of this book, then, is simply to teach the reader about the black bear, the most widely distributed bear in North America, and in doing so, help dispel any myths and untruths. Along the way, I hope the reader will realize what a marvelous, unique mammal the black bear is and that bears and humans *can* coexist.

Black Bear: Seasons in the Wild is best read aloud around a lively campfire—read loud enough so that any nearby bears can hear our interpretation of their remarkable lives.

For centuries, much of the bear's mysticism and allure to humans has stemmed from some of their humanlike characteristics such as the ability to stand upright. (Photo copyright by Michael H. Francis)

13

THE LEGENDARY
BLACK BEAR

If I really want to see a bear, all I have to do is step outdoors on a clear night, walk through the dark over to the edge of our hayfield, and direct my gaze skyward. The bear I seek on such nights has quietly moved since the birth of the heavens in tireless, ancient circles around the North Star, Polaris. My gaze is shepherded by the most recognizable group of stars in the Northern Hemisphere, the Big Dipper. And, if I widen my gaze as I study the dipper's seven familiar stars, I simultaneously gaze at its parent constellation, Ursa Major, otherwise known as the Great Bear.

It is puzzling to imagine how early sky watchers made out a bear among the dim stars. Perhaps to find the bear we must imagine an animal with a long tail (the four stars that make up the Big Dipper's handle). But that would be unlike any bear known since humans started writing bear tales and scratching figures of bears on the walls of caves. But interestingly, both the early Greeks and North American natives, separated by an ocean and a continent, identified the same collection of stars as a bear.

Bears have held major roles in the legends of many cultures around the world, and societal rules have been influenced by the mystique of the bear. Few animals have enjoyed the sacred, almost magical prestige that the bear has among most native peoples on the North American continent. "Bear medicine" was thought to be powerful and would not only help cure a multitude of ailments and offer protection, but also might provide visions that could help direct people toward secure, content lives. Such medicine might be found in a bear's paw that was decorated with beadwork or quillwork. Necklaces or bracelets made from the bear's claws were another form of medicine that protected or gave strength to the wearer. Even today, wild plants are used in herbal healing, and because many of them are favorite foods of bears, they are believed to be powerful healers. Some of these medicinal

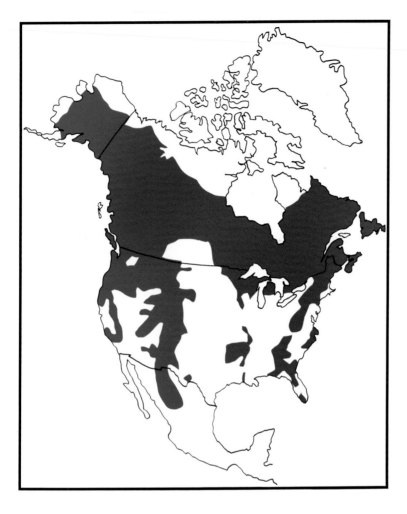

Above: Of the North American bears (the black bear, Ursus americanus; the grizzly or brown, Ursus arctos; and the polar bear, Ursus maritimus), none is more widespread or numerous than the black. Home for approximately 80 percent of the continent's estimated 750,000 black bears are the Canadian provinces and Alaska. A small number of black bears live as far south as the wilds of northern Mexico. The remaining bears live in the lower forty-eight states, primarily in the Pacific Northwest, the Rocky and Appalachian mountains, New England, and the Upper Midwest.

Imagine a range map that is almost entirely filled in. That's the way a century-old map would have looked, when much of North America was prime forested habitat, the black bear's favorite. (Map courtesy of Dr. Mike Pelton, University of Tennessee)

Right: Bears can claim dogs as close relatives. Taxonomists believe that dogs and bears had a common ancestor, an ancient animal referred to as "half dog," which bore features of both animals. This grazing bear's posture is reminiscent of our canine companion's form. (Photo copyright by Jeanne Drake)

plants have *bear* as part of their common name: bearberry (*Arctostaphalos uva-ursi*), bear grass (*Xerophyllum tenax*), and bear's garlic (*Allium ursinum*).

Other beliefs indicate that most North American natives treated the bear like a god. Though the black bear was hunted, its killing, butchering, and use had to follow a ritualistic set of rules. Among the Koyukon and Cree natives, of Alaska and Canada respectively, if these rules of respect were not followed, it was felt that the spirit of the killed bear would be unhappy and would speak of this lack of respect to other bear spirits still on earth. Those bears still roaming the forests would avoid the humans, making life difficult for the humans.

The easiest, and most preferred, way to kill a bear for these early peoples was to kill the bear during its hibernation. When an active den was discovered, its location could not be loudly broadcast, because the bear's spirit might be warned. Richard Nelson, in his fine book *Make Prayers to the Raven*, writes of the Koyukon people of central Alaska: "One man said that bears are very hard to find in their dens and their meat is extremely valuable, so people must treat them with the greatest respect. In other words, they need all the luck they can get, and the way to have luck is to show deference to their powerful spirits. And when he is ready to shoot a bear he should talk to it, telling where and how to move. For example, he might say, 'I am your friend' . . . 'be easy with me' . . . 'go slow' . . . 'put up your head.' Hearing this, the bear will obey."

Fascinating to the early natives was the bear's humanlike qualities. A bear oftentimes will stand erect on its two hind legs, making it appear like a standing human. Bears and humans eat the same kinds of foods: plants and meat. Consequently, it is easy to see why the early peoples felt bears to be "brothers and sisters" to human animals. Even bear and human skeletons are incredibly similar when in a standing posture. Both have long limb bones, a similar ribcage, a pelvic girdle, and a similar collection of digit bones in the paws and hands. However, the bear framework lacks a collarbone, and the snouted skull is equipped with a different set of teeth.

To gain legendary status is no small feat. The candidate must pass the test of time measured in generations rather than days or years. Ever since a black bear and a human met on this continent, there has been a connection between the two animals. This connection is in danger of being eroded as we distance ourselves from the natural world. We must remind ourselves that partnership with, not domination of, black bears is needed for a healthy, diverse menu of life. Have we lost the respect we once had for the bear, for things wild?

Legends are said to be immortal, but the black bear is one living legend over whose future we have complete control.

A snoozing black bear cub has a universal "teddy bear" appeal. Yet this "teddy bear" has the potential to grow into one of the largest carnivores in North America. (Photo copyright by Bill Lea)

THE BLACK
BEAR'S FORM

Due to its size, bulk, and usual mode of traveling on all fours, the black bear appears slow and clumsy. However, its speed, agility, and range of keen senses make this animal a marvelous collection of adaptations. (Photo copyright by Rick McIntyre)

I remember seeing a bear for the first time when I was on a Sunday drive with my parents. I was just a youngster. The black, shaggy beast we spotted from the car was some distance from us and was loping along the edge of a field, next to a woods. As we got closer and could better make out the animal's features, we discovered, much to our disappointment, that the bear was only a big, black farm dog. But for a brief moment we had shared our space with a "bear," and that alone made it a memory. No one forgets his first encounter with a wild black bear. First sightings of rabbits, frogs, and foxes are not as easily recalled as a first bear.

It's not all that surprising that we all thought the dog was a bear, and perhaps our mistake reflected the ancient bond these two animals once shared. Taxonomists believe that 25 million years ago, during the later part of the Oligocene epoch, bears and dogs belonged to a larger grouping, a superfamily of mammals we now call Canoidea, the "Doglike Ones." The Canoidea members, called "canoids," descended from an ancient group of flesh-eating animals called the "miacids," small animals that originated from early insect eaters. (The miacids are considered the forerunners of all the modern carnivores, although no miacids themselves survive today.) The Canoidea group comprised four subfamilies: Mustelidae (weasel), Procyonidae (raccoon), Canidae (dog), and Ursidae (bear). Those first bears were tiny compared to today's bears. They were predatory, fox-sized animals that shared a mountain-building and subtropical landscape with a host of primitive mammals, many of which have since faded into extinction, and some of which have become modern mammals.

With the passing of time through the Oligocene, the Miocene, and the Pliocene epochs, various forms of bears evolved and then died out. Some of these bears gradually increased in size, and

Above left: The "snow" or "ghost" bear is not an albino black bear but a white color phase of the black bear that is found in a relatively small area of rugged rainforest in northwestern British Columbia. This unique subspecies of black bear, commonly called the Kermode, was believed to be a distinct species of bear until 1928. White-phased Kermode females are capable of giving birth to black-phased cubs just as black-phased Kermodes might bear white-phased cubs. (Photo copyright by Art Wolfe)

Below left: The "glacier bear" is a steel-blue color phase of the black bear that lives in the coastal, heavily glaciated region of Alaska and northern British Columbia. Among black bears, the less common color phases, such as the blue phase, tend to be regional in distribution. (Photo copyright by Art Wolfe)

Right: Of the eighteen recognized subspecies of black bears, the most widespread is the black color phase. Color variations are more common in the western range of the black bear. (Photo copyright by Wayne Lankinen)

about 2.5 million years ago, a genus of very large bears called *Ursus* evolved in Europe. From this genus eventually came *Ursus etruscus*, which was the predecessor of three species: Two of these were, perhaps, the forebears of modern black and brown bears and immigrated to Asia; a third, *Ursus spelaus*, was the great eight-hundred-pound cave bear, which roamed the European continent for thirty thousand years until it mysteriously died off, perhaps due to disease, climatic change, or being over hunted by humans.

Those first bears that made their way onto the North American continent did so at about the start of the Pleistocene epoch (also known as the Ice Age), which dominated the Northern Hemisphere some 1.5 million years ago. During this time of surging and shrinking glaciers, much of the earth's water was in the form of ice, causing a lowering of the oceans, which occasionally dropped as much as ninety meters and exposed large expanses of land. One such uncovered plain connected Asia with North America; we now call it the Bering Strait. The early bears, along with other ancient mammals such as bison and wolves and even humans, crossed this land bridge that connected Siberia with Alaska; these bears were the ancestors of the modern black bear.

Half the North American continent was uninhabitable due to the expanse of thick ice sheets, so these early black bears lived in the southern regions of North America. Much later, perhaps only 100,000 years ago, the ancestors of the grizzly bear ambled across the exposed Bering Strait. Gradually, atmospheric temperatures started to rise, melting the gigantic ice sheets, filling the vast oceans, and covering exposed land such as the Bering Strait with water. The Pleistocene epoch came to an end, and evolution molded the bears into what we know today.

In North America live the black bear (*Ursus americanus*), the brown bear *(Ursus arctos)*, and the polar bear *(Ursus maritimus)*. The black bear is also commonly known as the American bear and lives only in North America; the brown bear, also known as grizzly bear and Kodiak bear, lives in western and northern North America as well as in much of Asia and into Europe; the polar bear is believed to have evolved from those brown bears that lived along the sea, and it now lives all along the frozen fringes of the Northern Hemisphere's continents and on its northern islands.

THE NAME OF THE BLACK BEAR
Common names of plants and animals often vary from region to region, but the Latin, or scientific, name is universal and changes only when taxonomists agree that a change is needed. Multipart titles make up scientific names, and often at least part of the name is based on some part of the animal's characteristics. The first part of the scientific name is the genus, a designation that places the animal in a general group of organisms that share similar characteristics. The second part is the species, so given because of the

Above: It is not unusual to see different color phases within a family of black bears. Here are black- and brown-phased siblings with their black-phased mother. Oftentimes, particularly among eastern populations, a brown-phased black bear will molt its brown coat for a black one as it gets older. (Photo copyright by Tom & Pat Leeson)

Overleaf: When bears are feeding together, much can be learned by observing their body language. Similar to a wolf, a bear will lay its ears back when threatened. Generally, black bears do not feed in groups (except for an adult female and her young), but when food is concentrated such as during a salmon spawning run, the bears will tolerate each other's presence. (Photo copyright by Tom & Pat Leeson)

25

animal's distinct identity. A third Latin name identifies the animal or plant as a subspecies.

For example, the black bear is known among taxonomists as *Ursus americanus*. The genus is the Latin word *Ursus*, which translates to "bear." The species name, *americanus*, is Latin for "of America," so given because it was in eastern North America that this bear was first described by European immigrants. A subspecies of the black bear is a white-phased bear commonly called the Kermode, *Ursus americanus kermodei*.

The honor of titling a "newly discovered" species of life with its scientific name is usually given to the species's "discoverer." This system of naming is sometimes misleading, however. The name *Kermode* is a good example. The name came about around the turn of the century when the bear was "found" by a naturalist who named it in honor of Francis Kermode, a British Columbian museum director. But in fact, the Northwest Coastal native people who lived near the white bear had known of the bear's existence for thousands of years, and still call the bear *"Moksgm'ol,"* among other names.

Because folks do not care to be burdened with Latin titles, we have common names for most flora and fauna. The common name *black bear* was an apt description for the bear that sixteenth-century European settlers encountered after arriving on the east-

This is a sedated black bear's front foot. Black bears are equipped with curved, almost catlike claws. Such claws enable the bear to climb trees more easily than any other North American bear. (Photo copyright by the Minnesota Department of Natural Resources)

Above: The grizzly bear's front claws are much longer than a black bear's claws and are not nearly as curved. Such claws are excellent tools for digging up foods such as plant tubers or ground squirrels. (Photo copyright by Rick McIntyre)

Right: The bear's keen ability to detect odors is legendary. A Native American phrase says it best: "A pine needle fell. The eagle saw it. The deer heard it. The bear smelled it." Like a dog, a bear extends its nose skyward to better catch subtle smells. (Photo copyright by Bill Lea)

The polar bear is an Arctic dweller and spends much of its life hunting over the treeless ice pack. Like the grizzly, it grows to a much larger size than the black bear. Besides its white color, the polar bear, or Nanook as the Inuit call it, has a long neck, a tapered head, and long legs. (Photo copyright by Jeanne Drake)

ern edge of the North American continent. The bear these early immigrants remembered from the old country was brown; when they met this glossy, black New World bear, its title was obvious. But, of course, the black bear was already known by the many Native American tribes. For example, the Crees of the Hudson Bay region refer to the bear as *"Muskwa"*; the Ojibway of the northern forests speak of the *"Maykwa"*; the Lakota know the bear as *"Wahconkseach Sapa"*; and the Koyukon of Alaska speak reverently of *"Sis."*

As the North American continent became more settled and men and women pushed their way west, early observers of this new home found bears of various colors and described them in journals. Undoubtedly, some of these bears were grizzlies, but many of them were different color phases of the familiar black bear. These and later observers found that black bears of the Canadian maritime provinces and of the eastern United States tend to be black. However, most western bears—particularly those found in the Rocky Mountain region—are rarely black, but are more likely colored in shades of chocolate to blonde browns, cinnamon to beige. Different explanations of the color variation have been suggested. Some biologists believe that black bears living in the Rocky Mountain regions endure hotter summer temperatures, and that a light-colored coat better reflects the sunlight. Brown coats, it would appear, are cooler in hot climates. However, nearly 100 percent of the bears living in the wet coastal forests of the Northwest are black, and another suggested explanation is that regional moisture levels dictate dominant color phase. Although a steel blue black bear inhabits only the coastal region of Alaska and the adjoining mountains of British Columbia, we do know that the various color phases are not strictly regional because a sow's new cub might be slightly different in coloration from its siblings. Also, before a black bear molts its winter coat in early summer, it might wear a pelage that is a sun-bleached brown. By the time it finishes molting its bleached, worn coat in mid-July, it will be wearing a glossy coat of black.

It is not known for sure, then, exactly what determines a black bear's color. Regardless of color phase, you'll be able to recognize the common characteristics shared by all black bears: straight muzzle profiles (almost doglike), slender faces, and the lack of a pronounced shoulder hump that is present in grizzlies.

THE SIZE OF THE BLACK BEAR

Of the three North American bear species, the black bear is the smallest. Although the heaviest black bear recorded was an impressive eight-hundred-pound animal shot in Wisconsin in 1985, it was nearly half the average weight of a large Alaskan brown bear, which might tip the scales at 1,500 pounds. For all species of bears, the male (boar) is typically larger than the female (sow).

Arriving at an average weight for the black bear is difficult, because there is a dramatic variation from spring to fall. Also, the bears' weight significantly varies among regional populations across the continent. However, the average weight of an adult (four years or older) male black bear usually falls between 250 and 450 pounds. Adult female black bears often weigh about half as much as the males, putting them in the range of 150 to 225 pounds. Excluding those black bear populations that feed heavily on migrating salmon along the northwestern coast of the continent, most western black bears tend to be slightly smaller than their eastern cousins. Larger eastern bears are not surprising because they frequent areas where human garbage and poorly stored camp or picnic foods are available. These robust bears have learned the rewards of scavenging on the sloppy habits of humans—much to the injury of the bears themselves.

When a black bear is on all fours, its shoulder is usually two to three feet off the ground. Its height, when the bear is reared up on hind legs, might measure six to seven feet. But a bear can seem bigger than it really is for several reasons. A bear's thick, long guard hairs—wear-resistant hairs in a mammal's coat—can increase the bear's apparent size. (The softer, shorter underfur is primarily an insulator, able to trap a greater amount of heat-holding air. The thicker the underfur, the better the animal is able to cope with cold temperatures.) In late summer and early fall, after a bear has accumulated a thick layer of fat, its rounded appearance also boosts its perceived size. The bear's size is further enhanced if it stands up on its hind legs, which it will do to better see its surroundings, just as we stand on our tiptoes to see over the heads of others in front of us at a summer parade. A standing bear is often misinterpreted to be a threatening bear, but it is most likely just wanting to get a better view or a better scenting and hearing vantage.

EVOLUTION'S GIFTS TO THE BEAR

The bear is able to stand up, thanks to its foot design. When dogs and bears diverged on their evolutionary journey, the canid's foot lengthened in the instep, making wolves and dogs faster and more energy efficient when running. The canids needed speed to catch prey. Biologists classify any animal that runs on its toes (digits), such as canids or members of the deer family, as "digitigrades." On the other hand, early bears and their descendants were not strictly carnivorous and depended on plant material for much of their diet. Obviously, they didn't need speed to chase down a berry-producing plant. Bears, raccoons, members of the weasel family, and humans walk and run flat footed rather than on their toes and are distinguished as "plantigrades." Because a bear runs flat footed does not necessarily mean that it is a lumbering animal. In a flat-out sprint, black bears have been clocked at better than

Grizzly bears, also known as brown bears, and brown-phased black bears might share the same fur color, but the grizzly bear has a distinct shoulder hump and a longer, doglike head with a jutting brow line. Where grizzlies and black bears share home ranges, the black bear usually avoids confrontations with its larger adult cousins. (Photo copyright by Rick McIntyre)

thirty miles per hour. Considering that the best of our Olympian sprinters might momentarily hit speeds of twenty-eight miles per hour, a healthy black bear would hit the tape first in every contest.

The black bear is further equipped to speedily climb trees, unlike the polar or grizzly bear. Though bears are not nearly as arboreal as squirrels, their claw design allows them to take to the treetops. Similar to a dog and unlike a cat, the black bear is unable to retract it claws. However, the bear's claws are somewhat catlike in that they are curved, enabling the claws to purchase a hold on the trunk of the tree. When a bear takes to a tree, it grasps the tree with its front feet and uses its hind feet to push itself upwards, giving the appearance of hopping up a tree. When coming down, the bear does so backwards until it gets close enough to jump to the ground. Cubs and yearlings are more apt to take to the trees than adults are simply because a tree offers some protection for them. When harassed, any black bear might retreat up a tree. It is not unusual to find black bears climbing into trees to feed on foods such as fruits and catkins, and bears might even climb trees to simply lounge in the limbs.

SENSES FOR SURVIVAL

Without question, the bear's strongest advantage in interpreting the world in which it roams and survives is its ability to detect the faintest of scents. Bears have been known to swim more than one-half mile across a lake to an island campsite where the source of beckoning, a camper's aromatic food supply, was found. Many similar incidents in which bears pinpointed a potential food source from several miles away have been documented. Humans have likely evolved in the opposite direction: Our sense of smell has become weaker as we have removed ourselves from hunting and food-gathering responsibilities. A finely tuned olfactory capacity is hardly necessary as we gather our plastic-clad or boxed food from the aisles of a supermarket.

Black bears, like most dogs, have long snouts. Within that snout is a sensory area approximately fifteen times more sensitive than humans'. The smelling ability of the bear is not only important in locating food but also allows a June male to locate a female as she approaches estrus, the period when she will ovulate and allow a male to mate with her. The bear's nose, with its abundance of smelling receptors, can pick up subtle, familiar odors that jog the bear's memory about past favorable or unfavorable experiences.

The bear's eyesight has always been considered to be the weakest sense. Though there remains much to be learned about a bear's vision, evidence indicates that a black bear has excellent close-range vision, that it has a range of color vision, and, apparently, bears are able to discern different shapes and sizes. Biolo-

Among the North American bears, the black bear is the most adept at climbing trees, and even without ladder-rung branches to aid in climbing, the black bear can take to the trees with amazing speed and agility. Tree climbing offers security and access to a more diverse food supply, such as catkins, berries, and nuts. This youngster is showing the typical form when descending a tree: It hugs the trunk with its front limbs and walks down the trunk with its hind legs in the lead. Other North American tree-climbing mammals, such as raccoons or squirrels, descend trees head first. (Photo copyright by George Wuerthner)

gists who have observed black bears foraging believe that the bear's peripheral vision is excellent. Some people mistake the bear's behavior of pretending to look away from a human or another bear as a clue of nearsightedness, but many biologists consider the bear's distant vision good. Canadian studies suggest that wild black bears use visual perceptions to identify and monitor threatening or nonthreatening intruders—human, bear, or otherwise.

A bear's rounded ears act as efficient funnels for gathering sounds, and its hearing ability might be twice as sensitive as a human's. There is some evidence that bears, like dogs, can detect high-pitched, ultrasonic sounds.

Though the bear does not have the tactile receptors that its ancient relative the raccoon has in its paws, its sense of touch is very keen in its lips. A bear's lips can delicately pluck ripe blueberries from a bush without tearing any of the foliage. In a sense, the bear's lips and tongue become fingers.

SPRINGTIME
EMERGENCE

"It is the season of youth, of beginning again; the season of blank pages, of unhurried time, of belief and optimism." Edwin Way Teale, *Wandering through Winter*

I don't believe there is a more abrupt transition between the four seasons than what occurs from winter to spring. This is the season that starts like a popcorn popper. Slowly, the world sizzles, then erupts with familiar signs of spring: the first pussy willows in the swamp, the first bluebird on the mailbox, or the loud flight of a solitary, fat bumblebee searching for a suitable underground nursery site for the coming year's brood. Each day we note a new change, but soon we cannot keep up, for the world is cutting loose as if every popcorn kernel bursts from seed to fluff at the very same moment.

Spring might be considered the season of new life, but for the black bear it is better described as the time of emergence. With the arrival of the spring equinox, the official pronouncement of the new season when the hours of daylight begin to outweigh the night hours, the black bear cubs are already two months old, veterans of the passing of winter.

The exact time that bears come out of their dens generally depends on where they live. Bears in the southern part of their range—southern United States—might emerge from their winter beds after denning for two midwinter months. Sometimes, if food is plentiful, the southern bears will not den up during the winter at all. Those bears in their northern range—northern United States and Canada—might den up for five months from October to March. But regardless of where they live, most black bears are out squinting into the spring sunshine by mid-April or early May. It is not certain which factors, or more likely which blend of fac-

Upon emergence in early spring, the cubs appear curious about the world outside their winter nursery. They soon practice the art of climbing as it is the cubs' primary means of defending themselves from threats. (Photo copyright by Michael H. Francis)

Above: What might appear as a winter yawn is likely a nervous or threatening gesture toward the den intruder. Such actions, combined with vocalizations such as huffs and blows, serve as visual and auditory signals that the bear's space is being threatened. (Photo copyright by Wayne Lankinen)

Right: Spring is a season of growth for both flowers and bear cubs. Though play is important for the growth of the cubs, the mother must remain constantly alert for potential trouble. (Photo copyright by Wayne Lankinen)

tors, trigger the spring awakening for bears. A change in air temperature, a longer day length, or even an early thaw that causes some flooding in low-lying dens might be reasons for the spring bear emergence.

The solitary, adult male usually emerges from his den before the mother and her cubs leave their winter shelter. After leaving his den, the male will not return. The mother and young, on the other hand, might spend the first few days near the den site and retreat to it if necessary. "Mom" lingers in the nursery den with her cubs, purchasing more time to give the cubs strength through her milk and to assure a later step into spring, when the conditions will be more favorable for her cubs to move about. After two

months in the den together, the mother and her cubs have established an inseparable bond. If the mother is accompanied by yearling bears, rather than cubs, they are likely to emerge earlier and will leave the denning area and casually move some distance to rest. After being cooped up in the den for a winter, the yearlings engage in some light play with one another.

Upon reentry into the bright world of spring, the bears appear dazed and somewhat sleepy. Bear biologist Craig McLaughlin notes that researcher Ralph Nelson describes bears as "walking hibernators" for a few weeks after they leave their dens because the bears require some time to switch from the physiology of denning to that of active foraging in the spring. In short order after the bears' emergence, the adult and juvenile bears, who are now at their lowest weight of the year, begin to feed. The food the bears find varies from region to region. Grazing is something we associate with brown-eyed bovines, but in much of their range, spring bears graze. Minnesota bear biologist Lynn Rogers notes that freshly sprouting grasses, sedges, and plants such as skunk cabbage make up over half of the Upper Midwestern bears' spring diet. Wooded lowlands and marshy edges are particularly good feeding areas in the early days of a bear's spring. Dave Garshelis, bear biologist for the Minnesota Department of Natural Resources, discovered as a graduate student working in Great Smoky Mountain National Park that the bears tend to be relatively inactive for much of the spring. He surmised that this might be an energy-conserving tactic, because most of the plants that the bears feed on at this time of the year are relatively low in nutrients. Therefore, the bears feed during a portion of the day and rest during the remainder.

Bears will also graze in trees. When the long, pendulous male catkins and the plumper, silvery female catkins appear just before leaf-out in early spring, bears often climb the tall, slender aspen trees and pull branches in to gather the high-protein flowers. To the hiker, torn aspen branches are good signs as to the feeding habits of a bear.

Throughout the seasons, whether her cubs are newborn or fifty-pound yearlings born the previous year, the sow remains diligent and always nearby her young. Rogers has noted that mother bears consistently rest near large trees. Such trees offer immediate sanctuary for the cubs or yearlings if they need to retreat up into the limbs. In the spring, the young cubs are primarily nourished by only their mother's milk, and by midsummer the cubs will have been weaned. However, there have been cases of a mother producing milk for her cubs into September. As the cubs grow older, they will experiment with food that they see their mother eat.

As spring advances, the insect world becomes busy. The days

Yearling bears, as well as cubs, find security by scurrying up a tree. (Photo copyright by Tom & Pat Leeson)

become longer and warmer, and the sunshine warms rocks, rotting logs, and large dome-shaped ant mounds built of gathered pine needles, grasses, and other debris. The warmth of these insect homes inspires the insects, such as ants, to begin their egg laying and pupae care. Black bears, over much of their range, seek these insects. In this way, the bear's early spring diet of plant material shifts to animal matter, and the bear shifts from grazer to predator.

Besides ants, bears are particularly fond of the larvae and nymphs of ground-nesting hornets and beetles. And during those years when the woods come alive with legions of army caterpillars that can strip a tree leafless with their constant feeding, bears feed well. If the spring is unseasonably cold, insect activity will slow or temporarily stop. Without insects, the bears are forced to look for other sources of food.

Besides preying on insects, the black bear will not overlook a chance to feed on a spawning run of suckers or other fish moving up a spring creek. Nor will the bear pass up a chance to eat a mouse discovered in a clawed-apart log or to kill a deer fawn lying still, trying to remain unseen. And, the black bear is not so finicky that it would ignore an opportunity to feed on the carcass of a road-killed deer, right next to the crows and ravens. There also exist those bears that learn of the sloppy habits of some human campers, picnickers, and homeowners. These are the bears that get into trouble because they become part of a conflict, yet they are guilty of only hunger. It is usually the human animal that is the more guilty party—of poor garbage-removal or food-storage habits. Scavenging, whether on found kills or garbage dumps, is an energy-efficient means of feeding, and very little work is done to accumulate some needed calories. It is obvious that the black bear survives because it is an incredibly opportunistic animal. It takes advantage of a variety of foods, depending on what is available. Dick Anderson, a training specialist with the Minnesota Department of Natural Resources, works in northern Minnesota, where garbage-raiding bears are not an infrequent problem. Anderson states, "There is nothing we eat that bears wouldn't eat!"

Throughout the spring, the mother bear and her cubs or yearlings roam through the mother's home range. A home range is an area used for most of the year and provides the food, water, and protection an animal requires. A home range is not necessarily defended. However, if a female with cubs encounters an adult male bear, she will send the cubs up a nearby tree, and she is oftentimes successful in driving the male away. An adult male bear will sometimes prey on cubs, which is enough incentive for a mother bear to chase him off. Even though the male might be much larger than the defensive female, she usually is aggressive enough to encourage him to withdraw.

A young bear learns from traveling and watching its mother. This youngster is experimenting in dissecting a log for the promise of insects such as ant eggs, larvae, or adults. (Photo copyright by Bill Ivy)

In the regions where a grizzly and a black bear might encounter one another, aggressive confrontations between the two species seldom develop. Through a series of posture and body signals, where one bear conveys recognition of another's dominance, the bears avoid actual confrontation. However, attacks between the two species have been recorded. In such cases, one might assume that the grizzly will dominate, but a large black bear might overpower a smaller, subadult grizzly.

Late in the spring, usually by mid-June, the bears begin to scratch themselves much as a dog might. They rub against trees, posts, or boulders in an attempt to remove their now ragged winter coat. Black bears molt once during the year, and an observant hiker might find the tattered remnants of the molt up until mid-July, when the molting usually ends.

THE MATING CYCLE

Spring moves on quietly until the bear's "love moon"; the month we call June. It's not love that one bear feels for another, but rather a mysterious, physical need to mate. Most likely, bears don't know that they are perpetuating their species when they mate.

Some black bear males are capable of breeding when they are one-and-a-half years old. Adult males are physically able to breed every year; however, in most populations, it is likely that only the larger, stronger, and dominant males do most of the mating. Female bears reach breeding maturity at different ages across the continent. If the sow is free of disease, in good physical shape, and of substantial weight she might be able to conceive between her second and third year. This has been found to be the case in Pennsylvania where Gary Alt, a long-time bear biologist, has studied black bears. He suspects the earlier breeding age is due to the abundance of food in the area. The litter sizes tend to be slightly larger there as well, and Alt occasionally comes across a litter of five cubs. In some parts of the continent, particularly in the north, where the growth rate is slower due to lesser food quality or abundance, the female might not bear her first litter until she is about seven years old.

With the approaching mating season, a mother bear who has yearlings lets them know that she will no longer tolerate their company. Through threatening vocalizations and more aggressive behavior, the female sends her offspring on their way, and the year-old bears strike out on their own. Now that the female is alone, she will be receptive to mating, and the two-year cycle starts over again.

The female's period of breeding readiness is known as the "estrus cycle." During the estrus cycle, a scent in the female bear's urine is left whenever she pauses to urinate, which is frequent,

Above left: During spring and summer travels, the cubs are never far from their mother. She is quick to discipline them if they dawdle or stray from her side. Note that as a bear strides, it steps fully on the sole of its foot rather than on just its toes. This flat-footed manner of walking is referred to as "plantigrade," as opposed to "digitigrade," which applies to an animal that is a toe-walker, such as a deer or a wolf. (Photo copyright by C. Allan Morgan)

Below left: During late spring and early summer, the bear begins to shed or molt its winter coat. Bears and other mammals often take on a scruffy appearance as they molt. Bears often choose to rub against trees, rocks, or even fence and sign posts to scratch off their shedding coats. (Photo copyright by Michael H. Francis)

and this scent indicates her readiness to mate to the noses of any roaming males. By advertising her breeding readiness ahead of time through her scent, the female will increase her chances of calling an adult male bear to her side when she most needs him for fertilization.

The male who has been lured might follow the female for several days, waiting for her to become receptive to his advances. During these anxious days, the male will not eat anything, nor will he waste time in napping. His focus is entirely on the female—unless another male happens upon the scene. If that happens, a brawl will likely result. Such fights can be bloody, and many male bears wear ragged scars about their necks and faces from such June battles. Sometimes, the "other" male will win. It is conceivable that the female might be inseminated by several males during her heat cycle. And it is just as likely that the resulting sibling cubs might have different fathers. Such a strategy ensures a greater genetic diversity and ultimately a stronger species.

Mating occurs repeatedly over a three- to four-day period when the female bear ovulates (when her unfertilized eggs are released from her ovaries). Biologist Dave Garshelis believes that if the female bear does not successfully breed during her estrus cycle, she is likely to come into estrus again within a month or so.

After fertilization, the embryo develops only slightly to the blastocyst stage. Rather than implanting itself on the uterine wall to continue development, the blastocyst floats free inside the uterus, and development of the embryo will not resume until later in the year. Biologists call this stage "embryonic delay"; embryonic delay's result is that the cubs are born and nursed in the winter den—in January or February. Their winter birth assures them ample time to grow before they have to support themselves on their own fat stores. Cubs developing within the mother's uterus cannot utilize the mother's fats very well, but once born, they can assimilate the fats in the milk more efficiently.

When the breeding season is finished and the chemistry of estrus has passed, the female will no longer be receptive to the male and will aggressively let her suitor know that his advances are no longer wanted. She roams in her home range while the male travels great distances with hopes of finding yet one more receptive female. If he cannot find more females, his duties as a papa bear are finished. Elsewhere in bear country, the yearlings, the older nonbreeding adults, and the mother bears with their young cubs shift quietly into summer.

Spring's flowers become summer's fruits, an important source of food for the bear. It is amazing how such a large and seemingly clumsy animal can so delicately remove the berries with its grasping lips and tongue. (Photo copyright by Rick McIntyre)

Reading Black Bear Sign

Black bears are creatures of the forest and usually go out of their way to avoid human contact. The bear's shy ways are protected by the lush, often impenetrable leaves, bushes, rocks, and streams as well as the forest's guardians—the blackflies, mosquitoes, and deer flies—that seek meals of blood. Thus, the bear is often quite secure in its attempts to live a quiet life. Those bears that live in areas where there is a fair amount of human activity tend to become more nocturnal in their travels, but if food is scarce in bear country, bears become more bold and will move about at midday. In remote areas, bears might be seen at any time of the day.

In order to witness a black bear in a wild setting well away from the temptations of garbage cans, open dumps, and heavily odored campsites, one must be lucky, patient, persistent, and skillful in interpreting the telltale clues that a passing bear leaves behind. Such a skill in deciphering tracks, droppings, diggings, or even a shed hair was known among early nineteenth-century beaver-seeking mountaineers as "readin' sign." Admittedly, there are few instances when you would actually want to follow a black bear, unless you are a bear biologist interested in learning the ways of bears, a bear hunter, a wildlife photographer, or just a boldly curious naturalist.

Ernest Thompson Seton, a well-known artist, naturalist, and author in the first half of the twentieth century, was skillful in deciphering the clues left by passing animals. He realized that most wildlife knowledge does not come from watching the animal; it comes from reading the animal's life story in its tracks, scat, and markings—its "sign." "As with the Indian, the naturalist also must acquire some measure of proficiency in the ancient art [of reading sign]. Its usefulness is perennial to the student of wildlife; without it he would know little of the people of the wood." So it is with black bears; we can learn a great deal more of their lives if we learn to look for their clues.

The most obvious clue left by a passing bear is its track. Most field guides dealing with track interpretation fall short in describing or showing an animal's track because the impressions can vary tremendously. Soil or snow consistency, air temperature, and exposure to the sun are among the factors that can alter a track to the point that it becomes unrecognizable.

A bear's feet are distinctive. Its front feet are large and flat footed, with five toes; the back feet have a large heel pad behind the five toes. Bear tracks can hardly be confused with any other animal's. The average length of a black bear's hind foot track is five to seven inches (including the claw imprints); the average width is three to four inches. The smaller front print is approximately four inches by four inches. Rarely will you find the impres-

For its size, the black bear is amazingly elusive in its forested home range. Most views, such as this one, will be from a distance. It is more likely that we will encounter bear sign, or clues, such as tracks, droppings, diggings, and scratchings. (Photo copyright by Michael H. Francis)

Above left: Wild fruits, such as these black cherries, are favorite bear foods when they occur in the bear's home range. During the years when wild foods are abundant, the bear is able to feed well without having to range over greater distances. During lean years, bears often resort to raiding trash cans or campsites and might roam into residential areas in search of food. (Photo copyright by Bill Lea)

Below left: By investigating a bear's scat, one can determine what the bear has recently fed on. Here we can see the large, indigestible seeds from black cherries. If the bear has fed on fruit, such as berries, the color of the berries will show up in the droppings. (Photo copyright by Bill Lea)

Right: When feeding on berry-laden trees, a bear reaches up, grasps a branch, and pulls it down to mouth level so that it might more easily eat the fruit. Torn branches on favorite food trees are good clues to the presence of bears. (Photo copyright by Bill Lea)

sion of the heel pad in a front foot track because the bear puts its forward weight on its toes. And, because the bear's front claws are longer than its rear claws, the black bear's front foot toe tracks are often tipped with claw impressions (although definite claws marks are not always visible). If you are fortunate enough to find a series of tracks, you will be able to "read" the gait of the bear. In a steadily moving, relaxed bear, the tracks will appear in staggered pairs. Each pair of tracks is made up of a hind and front footprint, with the hind track directly in front of the forefoot track.

If you are traveling in country where both grizzlies and black bears are found, differentiating the two species' tracks can be difficult. Generally, a grizzly track is larger than a black bear print. Grizzlies' claws, measuring one and one-half to four inches on the front foot, are also much longer than a black bear's, which measure only one to two inches in length. In *Bear Attacks*, author Stephen Herrero states that the toes of a black bear show a greater tendency to arc, like a compressed crescent, whereas the grizzly's toes appear in a more distinct straight line. Another characteristic Herrero points out is that the black bear's toe impressions are usually separate from each other, while the grizzly's toe prints are often joined. But be aware of the consistency of the soil or snow when making these distinctions.

Because bears are nearly insatiable eaters during the summer and early fall, they leave ample sign in the form of droppings or scat. Yes, a bear does "dump in the woods," and trained eyes can find predictable places to locate such bear clues. Look for scat in clearings, on game and human trails (much to the chagrin of hikers and portagers), and even on roads. By perfecting your skills in scatology, you can determine how recently the scat was deposited, what kinds of foods the bear has been dining on, and the area the bear has been frequenting. If the scat is moist, it is fairly fresh; as it ages, it dries out. Insects are often attracted to fresh scat. Some, such as flies, will choose to lay their eggs on the droppings. And some insects, such as yellow swallowtail butterflies, will flutter above fresh bear scat, alight, uncurl their rolled proboscises, and feed off the bear waste. These dainty insects are likely in search of various amino acids available in the scat.

Examine any scat you may find in the woods, using a stick as a probe, and try to determine the animal from which it came. No other animal of the forest has scat that so closely resembles that of a human (although it is difficult to tell grizzly and black bear scats apart). More than once I have heard people, upon returning from an outing, utter disgust at the slovenly habits of some campers or hikers. Little did they realize that they were witness to a black bear toilet. If you are lucky enough to find bear scat, look for any food parts that the bear was unable to digest, such as seeds, nut parts, berry skins, insect parts (the insect's exoskeleton is primarily chitin, a hard undigestible covering), fish scales, or ani-

With their curved claws, bears can make quick work of peeling back the bark of a tree. This lashing bear is likely gaining access to a gallery of insects. Ants, beetles, and other tree-living insects are an important part of the bear's spring and summer diet. (Photo copyright by Michael H. Francis)

52

mal hair. If the bear has been feeding on meat, the droppings will be nearly black and carry an odor. If the bear has been feeding on rotting carrion, the droppings will be runny. If the bear's diet is primarily vegetarian, there will be little detectable odor, but a largely berry or fruit diet might result in a runny stool as well. During the height of the blueberry season, often skins of blueberries are within the scat, and it is often shaded a distinct purple to blue color. Obviously, the better you familiarize yourself with the fruits and nuts of a region, the better you will be able to successfully "read between the scats." If you find scat with bits and pieces of plastic packaging, food labels, and so on you know you have come upon a bear that is learning to associate food with humans. DO NOT camp in an area where such droppings are found.

Other easy-to-spot signs are sites where a bear has been searching for insects, grubs, homes of ground-nesting wasps, and fruit. You might come across rotting logs or stumps that have been torn apart, stones that have been shoved aside, or diggings where the bear has been hunting. Evidence of the bears' searches for fruit, ramblings and tearings in trees and shrubs, can be found. Bears may have to climb well up into a tree to reach the desired food, such as springtime aspen catkins, and in doing so will leave a trail of broken and hanging limbs. When feeding in blueberry or raspberry patches, bears do not move as gracefully as do human pickers. The bushes will likely show signs of trampling, and some of the shrubbery will be torn. They generally do not pick every ripe berry from the plant, because they are in a hurry to move on to the next clump of berries. In agricultural areas, bear sign can be found in tattered corn stalks, flattened oats, or in a plundered bee yard. When a black bear feeds on a large mammal carcass, or in the rare occasion that it kills another mammal, such as a fawn or even another bear, the dead animal's skin will be left uneaten and turned inside out.

Bears monopolize what food is available. Chances are that most of the bears in a particular area will be feeding on the same types of food at the same time of the year. Trampled trails and feeding sites become obvious clues of the bears' habits. Bear biologist Wayne McCrory notes that in areas were black bears densities are good, bear pathways are common. In such areas, the bears might leave a complicated network of trails that include main travel lanes and subtrails leading to bedding or feeding sites. Bedding sites are not often encountered. They tend to be bowl shaped, similar to a deer bed; if you come across a nest of dry leaves or needles, you might find some long, coarse black hairs. Often, the nests are located under large, overhanging trees or under rock shelves. In some regions, it is not unusual to discover small bear wallows or bear "tubs" in the forest. These wet depressions might offer the bear some relief from insects or heat.

If you are fortunate on your bear-search ramblings, you might

In the western coastal states and provinces, black bears often peel away the outer bark of trees to get to the sought-after cambium layer (inner bark). Humans and bears often clash in regions where logging and tree-feeding bears occur. To the human, the tree provides income; to the bear, the same tree offers food. (Photo copyright by Tom & Pat Leeson)

come across what is known as a "bear tree" or "rubbing tree." Biologists believe that the principal function of these trees is a scent marker. Most trees are marked during the spring-summer breeding season. They might serve as locations for scent trails of sexually active bears, and evidence shows that both sexes will visit such trees during the breeding season.

Most bear trees are located where they have the best chance of being seen and smelled by other bears, usually near a well-established bear travel route. Heavily used routes are more likely found in communal bear feeding areas such as a lush berry patch, a grove of acorn-producing oak trees, an open dump, or a fishing site. Male bears are most often the creators of such trees. A male might rake his claws along the tree's trunk, strip away the bark, and bite at the tree. It will also rub against the tree, either to leave its scent for other bears or to merely scratch itself. In a sense, the bear is leaving its signature. If you look closely at such trees you will probably find tufts of hair. However, this type of bear tree should not be confused with the occasional tree that a bear will rub against during the molting of its fur. Boulders, fence posts, and downed logs are often used to rub against during the annual molt.

A peeled tree trunk is another clue of a bear's presence. Much to the chagrin of the logging industry, black bears, particularly in the northwestern states and in British Columbia, will strip off the outer bark of certain coniferous trees in order to feed on the inner bark known as the cambium layer.

In honing your skills in finding bear clues, you will begin to unlock the comings and goings of the bear as well as other creatures that share its forest home.

Left: The pronounced arc of the front toes and less distinct claw imprints tell us that this trackmaker was a black bear. The track of the hind food would be longer, with a distinct print from the heel pad. We could guess at the bear's weight by interpreting its track, but our judgment might be wrong if we don't consider the consistency of the snow, mud, or dirt medium. (Photo copyright by Michael H. Francis)

Right: As with other grazers and foragers, bears are selective about the plants and fruits they feed on. We don't know whether bears prefer the tastes or somehow know which foods will bring the greatest benefit to their health. (Photo copyright by Michael H. Francis)

A BLACK BEAR SUMMER

"The big woods are hot and dry and quiet these days, for we have come to summer's halfway mark and nature is pausing for a rest on the portage from spring to fall." John Rowlands, *Cache Lake Country*

The change from spring to summer passes in a subtle and quiet moment. There is no grand proclamation "Summer!" The days are longer, the countryside tempered. We humans celebrate summer quietly, trying to avoid working up a sweat. We spend more time watching for the dance of a fishing bobber, sitting in a tree's shade and eating ice cream, lying in the shallows of a lake and letting the rhythm of the waves caress us; or we might, in a burst of energy, pack in as many activities as we can through the long, sunlit days.

Black bears are not much different from us in their celebration of summer. As the days become hotter, the bears take on a more nocturnal pattern of activity because it is cooler and more comfortable at night. Though there might be nighttime mosquitoes to deal with, the daytime bloodseekers such as deerflies or blackflies are absent. A bear's summer coat offers some help in fending off mosquito probes, but the burrowing, biting flies persistently work their way down to the bear's skin. Bears might take to a stream, lake, or mudhole to cool down and avoid the insects. A coating of mud plastered over the bear's fur adds another protective layer against pesty insects.

Early summer finds the cubs shedding their "cub" fur. From this point on, they will start growing into their winter fur. During the warm spring, the sun might have bleached the cubs' first coat, transforming black-phased cubs into lighter-colored browns and cinnamons. As the cubs molt the bleached hairs, the new ones will usually be contrastingly dark. By this time, the cubs will have grown their first permanent teeth, and when they den up in the

Left: Though the summer world might seem sultry and slow and lazy, it is a season when the bear must earnestly explore the countryside for the foods needed to accumulate fat for the upcoming winter. This beaver pond might serve as a cooling-off place, or the plants and animals that live here might provide food. (Photo copyright by Bill Ivy)

The cubs stay under the protection of their mother through the summer, and the mother bear is steadfast in the protection of her cubs from other bears. Normally, she would send her cubs up a nearby tree, but in this case no such security is available, so she confronts an approaching bear while her cub watches. Most encounters result with the intruding bear being successfully driven off. (Photo copyright by Tom & Pat Leeson)

fall, they will have all of their permanent teeth except for their long canine teeth, which will erupt over the winter.

Though the cubs will dutifully follow their mother into summer, they could, in the event of their mother's death, be self-sufficient at six months of age. However, their chances for survival are best under the care of their mother. Typically, the mother bear and her cubs will avoid other bears. Adult male bears sometimes kill cubs and yearlings, and, if an adult male bear or some other threat is encountered, the mother bear will give a vocal command that orders the cubs to climb a tree for safety. If a cub ignores its mother or isn't responding as fast as she would like it to, she will use a combination of commands or an aggressive swat to get the message across.

Over the course of the summer, the cubs become less and less dependent on their mother's milk. They learn from their mother which berries, leaves, roots, and insects to search for and eat. The cubs will learn from sampling; if they are reinforced with a reward (food), they will likely repeat the effort. Those cubs and yearlings that consistently find a dump or a series of garbage cans will likely develop into what some folks disdainfully call "dump" or "garbage" bears. In those areas where beekeepers are trying to bank on honey, bears might invade the apiary for a meal of both honey and insect, particularly the cream-colored larvae. As bears boldly search for food in areas close to humans, we experience a rise in so-called "nuisance" bear reports. Unfortunately, such reports usually result in the premature death of a bear.

With summer comes a smorgasbord for black bears. During the passing of summer, various berry crops such as raspberries, blackberries, blueberries, and pincherries ripen. Summer is also the season when insects are at their maximum numbers. Though evidence shows that bears consume more insects in late spring and early summer, they continue to take advantage of the situation when a meal of insect larvae presents itself. Ants, beetles, caterpillars, and even honey bees or wasps are all potential bear food. If there is a concentrated food source, such as an expanse of blueberries or a river full of salmon, a number of bears might gather to feed. At this time of the year, bears gather to seek food, not companionship, and bears might travel great distances to a particular food source. However, a female with cubs does not travel as fast nor as far as those bears without the anchor of cubs.

The yearling bears who were cut off from their mother earlier in June are finding out for themselves what the world is like. During this period they try to find a vacant piece of the forest to take as their own home range. Yearling females tend to establish home ranges within their mother's home range, and it is likely that mother and daughters will encounter each other in future travels or feeding forays throughout their lives. Such meetings are usually tolerated by the mother and her daughters. Male yearlings tend

Right: This bear is shaking off summer's heat by taking to the water for a cooling dip. The water not only makes summer more tolerable, but also it gives momentary relief from bothersome insects such as deer flies or mosquitoes. (Photo copyright by Rick McIntyre)

Overleaf: When the opportunity presents itself, the bear will take advantage of the moment. This bear is feeding on an elk carcass that it discovered. Viewing this scene, we might mistakenly assume that the bear was the predator, when in reality it was a scavenger, a role it shares with crows, magpies, coyotes, and many other animals and birds. Though it is very rare that bears kill adult elk or deer, they have been known to kill fawns. (Photo copyright by Tom & Pat Leeson)

to roam farther, sometimes well beyond their mother's home range. By moving farther out, these young males lessen the likelihood of breeding with their mother or sisters. Upon dispersal, a yearling might find itself in the home range of an adult male bear who might kill the trespasser, particularly if it is a male. Evidence indicates that cannibalism does exist in the world of the black bear, particularly at times of food shortages.

The highest risk of mortality for a black bear is during the first few months of its life. This is when the youngster is at risk of many dangers, including being killed by a larger black (or grizzly in grizzly country) bear. Another critical time for a young bear is its period of dispersal, when the yearling leaves its mother. The bear is on its own for the first time and perhaps not yet completely wise about perils it faces, such as a greater likelihood of being hit by a motor vehicle while attempting to cross roadways that traverse bear country. The yearling might also be more tempted to follow enticing scents found around humans and find itself raiding garbage cans. Unfortunately, many of these bears are shot as nuisance bears.

As summer creeps towards fall, a bear's priority becomes eating. The season of crisp air and brilliantly colored foliage is when the bear must finish accumulating winter's calories in preparation for a long winter sleep.

Above left: Summer is a season of play for bear cubs. The cubs spend much of their time tumbling and wrestling with each other. There is much value in play; it not only sharpens their coordination, but also it helps develop muscles that will later be needed for the bears' survival. (Photo copyright by Bill Ivy)

Above: Along the coastal regions of Alaska and Canada, black bears gather to fish along rivers where salmon migrate upstream to spawn. During such periods when food is abundant, it is important that the bear feeds heavily and often. Once the salmon quit running, the bear might find leaner times in its domain. (Photo copyright by Tom & Pat Leeson)

In the Wilds with a Black Bear

We had returned to our remote campsite following an evening of fishing. After pulling our canoe out of the water, my two friends and I discovered that our camp had been ransacked. Our food pack, which we had foolishly left next to the picnic table, was a mess, and our tent had a new tear in the back door. Left behind was a trail of bread leading some yards to the empty bread bag, which seemed to indicate that our return had frightened the camp robber off.

The evidence overwhelmingly suggested that a bear had visited, but each of us hoped aloud that the job was done by a very ambitious raccoon or two. After cleaning up the mess, we retreated to the torn tent, crawled into our sleeping bags, and with false bravado convinced ourselves that the vandal would not return that evening. After the usual presleep banter in the tent, we quieted down.

I can't speak for my companions, but in those silent moments when sleep evaded me, my mind played host to numerous bear scenarios, of which none was particularly pleasant. For the first time in my life, I slept with my fillet knife. It didn't matter to me that such a feeble weapon would likely get me into trouble by only injuring or irritating the bear. Sometimes fear has a way of making us irrational. Nevertheless, the knife's presence comforted me a little bit.

Suddenly, something was rearranging our silverware and cook kit outside. With heart in mouth, Mike, lying closest to the tent window, quietly got out of his sleeping bag and directed his flashlight out the window. His declaration was not a surprise: "It's a bear—a big one."

The combination of the flashlight and the excited, squeaky-voiced noises from inside the tent was enough for the bear, and in an instant it was gone. There was no clumsy crashing through the underbrush. It was as if the bear had been an illusion; here and gone in a silent moment.

Convinced that the bear would not return knowing that we were lying in our tattered, canvas fortress, we settled down after renewed exchange of bedtime chatter. Sleep was a stranger that night, and finally my vigil paid off when I heard a shuffling by my head, just on the other side of the canvas. In the next moment, I realized that my two friends had been pretending to sleep, because we all started yelling. For a second time the bear quietly exited.

Enough was enough. In a matter of minutes, under the glow of a hissing lantern, we hurriedly stuffed our sleeping bags and piled the unfolded tent into the canoe. With two of us paddling and the third holding the shining lantern over the bow, we made our way in the dark, early morning hours to a small rocky island,

The black bear is often mistakenly considered one of the greatest pests and threats to humans who escape to the woods to camp. Bear and human conflicts most often arise when humans inadvertently attract bears to their campsites because of sloppy kitchen habits. (Photo copyright by Michael H. Francis)

Though this bear has never heard that it should keep its feet off the table, it has learned that campgrounds are the sources of tasty treats such as a carelessly abandoned can of beans. Such conditioned bears are quickly labeled "nuisance bears," yet it is ironic how many people will purposely leave food out with the hopes of attracting a bear. Who is the real nuisance? (Photo copyright by James H. Robinson)

where we spent the remainder of the night.

After sunrise, we returned to the battered campsite to pick up the rest of our gear and salvage what food we could find. It was obvious that the bear had returned after we made our getaway. Luckily, we planned on returning to civilization on that day, so the loss of food was minimal, and there was enough oatmeal to nourish us for the return trip.

Unfortunately, such bear encounters are often the first or the only experiences campers or picnickers have with black bears. Scores of such incidents happen every year and will continue to happen unless proper precautions to minimize bear visits are taken. Some of these encounters can lead to human injury when campers become careless. Always avoid campsites that show any recent bear signs such as messages from previous campers, fresh bear scat, or scattered food packaging. I recall a trip into the canoe country of northeastern Minnesota when we pulled into shore at an established scenic campsite. Everything looked perfect, until we saw the large white letters B . . E . . A . . R poured onto the slope. The previous campers had poured the warning using flour as a printing medium. Needless to say, we paddled on.

Most campers who are raided by a bear actually invite bears into camp. Black bears quickly learn that humans are the sloppiest creatures in the woods. Bill Peterson, Area Wildlife Manager for the Minnesota Department of Natural Resources in the heart of prime bear country in northeastern Minnesota, hears reports of many nuisance bears each year. Peterson bluntly states, "You will eventually encounter bears if you practice sloppy camping habits."

Minimum-impact camping will help lessen the likelihood of a snooping bear. Simply put, a clean camp is perhaps the most important preventive in keeping your camp bear free. Do not throw leftovers off in the brush or latrine. Pick up every scrap, noodle, and morsel of leftover or spilled food. Do not pour grease in the bushes next to your camp; burn it. Wash all dirty pots and dishes immediately after eating, and then dump the dishwater on land well away from camp. The camp cook often has grease spattered on his or her clothes; hang clothes tainted by food smells outside the tent well out of a bear's reach. Any garbage that cannot be burned, such as cans and bottles, should be cleaned or burned out and finally stored in a plastic bag and packed out.

Never leave any food or garbage unattended in camp. Even if you leave for a short hike, hang it up or store it in a way that will not invite a bear into camp. Your food supply should be packed in plastic bags or containers, which help to minimize the escape of telltale odors. The U.S. Forest Service recommends that the food packs be hung at least twelve feet off the ground from a stout branch or pole and no closer than ten feet from the nearest tree trunk. The Forest Service also suggests that it is best

to tie the packs in a bola fashion, with one pack tied at each end of the rope. This way, the two packs counterbalance each other, and they needn't be tied to the ground or a nearby tree with a rope that a bear can chew through, leading to a midnight snack. When retrieving the pack, use a long stick to push one of the packs up, thus lowering the second pack to within reach.

Not everyone agrees with the Forest Service's advice. Cliff Jacobson, wilderness canoe guide and author of several camping books, has never had a bear tear into his food packs in thirty-five years of camping. Jacobson might hang his gear on occasion, but for the most part he stores food in plastic bags and containers and places the scent-free food packs some distance away from camp, well off of any established trails. "Bears," Jacobson notes, "become creatures of habit and will not only follow worn trails but also learn from which trees campers tend to hang their packs. Even if the bear cannot reach your hanging pack, it's not easy sleeping through a bear's noisy attempts, particularly if that pack is hanging next to your tent!"

Some campers think the moat of water that encircles an island will keep bears away. But consider a case in which some canoeists stowed their food supply in an anchored canoe out from shore. They learned that bears are excellent swimmers and that they will swim out for the promise of a meal!

In the bear encounter that I mentioned, my friends and I came away from the trip with a torn tent. The reason: A candy bar had been left in a clothes pack. We learned never to leave any food items in the tent. If we had left flaps to the tent open, the bear could have investigated the candy bar without having to tear a hole in the tent wall. When away from your campsite, it might be a good idea to permit access to your tent for the overly curious bear.

The same preventive measures apply to car-camping. However, rather than hanging your food supply out of reach, keep it closed up in the trunk of your car or inside your vehicle. It's still a good idea to keep food wrapped and sealed to lessen the chances of a bear sniffing it out.

Unfortunately, our sloppy camping practices of that fateful night years ago might have drawn in a previously innocent bear and we might have unknowingly created a "problem bear," a bear that might have very well learned the rewards of campsites for the promise of a meal. Such actions not only jeopardize the bear's future but also put other campers as greater risk of being injured by a bear.

Left: Of the North American bears, humans more commonly encounter the black. The likelihood of a hostile encounter with a black bear is remote, however. The bear will more likely bluff, trying to intimidate rather than attack, and actual bear attacks are exceedingly rare. When they do happen, they are front-page news and bear phobia spreads quickly. But note that bears are wild animals, and treat every bear encounter as if it has the makings of injury. (Photo copyright by Tom Walker)

To lessen the odds of a bear ambling into your campsite, practice minimum-impact camping, reducing any opportunity for a bear to find food or scents of food. (Photo copyright by Jeanne Drake)

THE BLACK BEAR'S
AUTUMN

"Fall belongs to the hunter, if for no other reason than winter demands it." Guy De La Valdene, *Making Game*

Suddenly, almost abruptly, summer passes into autumn. The days noticeably shorten, the temperatures drop, and the leaves of the birch and wild sarsaparilla flush with yellow. Snowshoe hares begin to molt their summer brown hairs, which are replaced with white hairs that eventually will help them blend into the winter landscape. Flocks of white-throated sparrows frantically move through the thickets as they work their way south. Even the evening autumn sky reflects this urgency to move on. Nighttime migrants such as warblers, thrushes, and vireos chirp below the stars as they keep in contact with each other while moving through the darkness. The ponds and lakes cool down, giving rise to ghostly mists in the day's first light; soon they will be locked in ice.

Fall brings with it a real sense of urgency. Though black bears are not in tune with a twelve-month calendar, they are very much aware of their seasonal needs, and the need for more and more calories continues without pause from summer to fall. This is the season when bears gain up to a third of their body weight. Biologists refer to this state of frenzied feeding as "hyperphagia." According to nutritionists, the average adult human male consumes approximately 2,500 calories per day. In the fall, a hyperphagic black bear might take in 20,000 calories per day. To eat such quantities, bears often feed beyond the daylight hours, and early autumn finds bears seeking more food than sleep. There will be plenty of time to rest later.

Autumn is viewed as a season of plenty, a season of harvest. Calorie-rich acorns from the oaks have filled out and finally drop

With autumn comes the familiar filled-out figure of the bear. This is the season that they must finish accumulating the fuel of fat needed to survive the coming winter. The bear ambles through fall doing little other than consuming calories. (Photo copyright by Tom Walker)

to the ground. Squirrels, chipmunks, white-footed mice, and even blue jays can be seen carrying off acorn prizes to cache for the possible lean days ahead. Wood ducks, wild turkeys, whitetail deer, and black bears are also fond of this autumn manna. Black bears that live in areas where acorns are available will gain weight faster than bears that live in oakless forests. For over ten years, the Minnesota Department of Natural Resources has been conducting a black bear study in a 120-square-mile area in northern Minnesota. Project leader Dave Garshelis and his research team have placed radio collars on more than three hundred bears and have tracked the animals' seasonal movements. Project research biologist Karen Noyce said that during those years when there is a good acorn crop, black bears in the study area will "oftentimes travel twenty to fifty miles to areas where they feed on the acorns." Apparently, the bears remember these oak pantries, because many of them return to the same areas in subsequent years. In some parts of the continent, salmon rivers or berry patches have the same magnetism for voracious bears.

The bear's pelage becomes thick and carries a lustrous sheen with the approach of winter. Native Americans and early European settlers sought the thick bearskins to use as warm sleeping covers and as winter robes and coats. To this day, members of various regiments of the Royal Guards in England wear impressive hats called Busbys made from the fur of black bears, which is most likely imported from Canada because black bears are not native to Britain.

For most black bears, autumn comes to an end when the time to hibernate comes, about mid-October. Bears that live in the more northerly latitudes or in higher elevations tend to den up earlier than their more southerly counterparts. Bears living in southern New England, mid-Atlantic, and northwestern states often delay denning until well into November. Other than pregnant female bears, most Floridian bears do not den up for the winter.

But bears within a region don't all den up at the same time. Researchers speculate that an individual bear might vary its denning time from year to year depending on food availability in the summer and fall as well as the bear's physical condition. Several studies have shown that in some areas pregnant females hibernate earlier than other bears. Those bears that have put on ample fat stores, a layer that might be four inches thick, tend to hibernate before leaner bears. Female black bears, with or without cubs, tend to den up before the males. And of the males, it appears that the younger males are last to hole up.

A few days prior to denning up for the winter, bears rest and drink plenty of water. It is believed that this behavior cleans the bear's system. Pregnant females tend to winter in more carefully built dens such as those found under root systems of downed

Before the bear dens up, it drinks great quantities of water. Some researchers believe the drinking helps to clean the bear's system. Once the bear is in hibernation, it will not have another drink of water until it leaves its den. (Photo copyright by Rick McIntyre)

Left: This fattened bear assumes a comical position as it uses three of its feet to consider a pine cone for an autumn snack. For their bulk and brawn, bears can be deceptively gentle in their handling of food. (Photo copyright by Tom Walker)

Above right: Nature's oldest rule, "survival of the fittest," could be altered to "survival of the fattest" for those animals that have to cope with the lean months of winter. (Photo copyright by Michael H. Francis)

Below right: Prime feeding areas will draw bears from miles, but the farther a bear has to travel, the more calories it burns—calories it will need throughout its denning time. (Photo copyright by Michael H. Francis)

trees or within jumbles of boulders. Rarely do two or more bears—other than mothers and cubs or yearlings—use the same denning site, unless there is a shortage of suitable sites. This might occur in areas where rock dens are most often used, sites that are at a premium. In the Great Smoky Mountain National Park area, black bears seem to prefer to den up in large, hollowed-out trees. In some areas, particularly in the lush forests of the Pacific Northwest, black bears will den in hollow old-growth conifers that measure up to ten feet in diameter. Even in the north, some bears will depart from autumn by merely scraping a nest of leaves, grasses, and mosses on top of the ground within the cover of the branches of a wind-downed tree. The inevitable blanket of snow will provide the bear's quilt.

Now, after the pregnant female bear goes into hibernation, the undeveloped bear embryos (blastocysts), which have remained dormant for months, finally and mysteriously implant themselves on the wall of the female's uterus and resume normal growth.

And while autumn might begin on a frantic note, it ends for the black bear in a quiet stupor. The harvest is in, and now it is time to rest.

Above: Most twentieth-century taxidermied bears or bear artwork portray bears standing on hind legs, giving them an appearance that is to humans more threatening. As a result, when standing bears are encountered in the wild, they are perceived as dangerous, when actually they are likely raising themselves up for a better view. (Photo copyright by Michael H. Francis)

Right: The summer petals of wild roses have dropped, and now the fruit, rose hips, are left for this bear to harvest. The bear's clawed foot rakes the shrub closer before its lips delicately pluck the fruit from the plant. (Photo copyright by Michael H. Francis)

Coming Face to Face
with a Bear

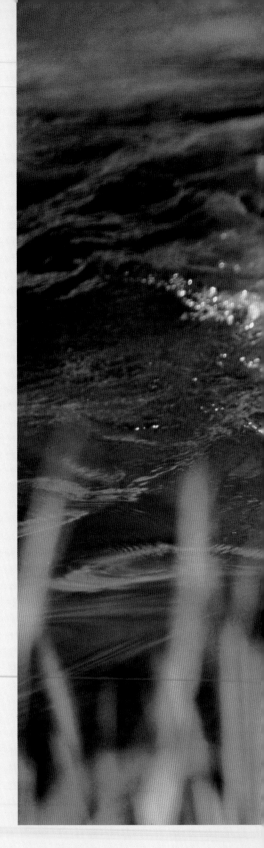

It was during a ten-day canoe trip in September of 1987 that Minnesotans Jeremy Cleaveland and his twenty-nine-year-old son, James, were interrupted by an unusual bear. After some early morning fishing, the Cleavelands returned to camp for a breakfast of pancakes and bacon. After eating, the men began breaking camp to move on to another campsite. Just minutes before they were to shove off, James said, "Look Dad, there's a bear!" A smallish bear came out of the woods and ambled toward the campers. Pots and pans were already packed, so rather than beat on them to make noise, the men yelled and waved their arms. At thirty yards, the bear stopped and paced back and forth.

Because the canoe was nearly loaded, James grabbed the food pack and stowed it so they could be off. Unexpectedly, the minute James went out of sight, the bear boldly loped toward Jeremy. Jeremy yelled and, waving his arms, threw water on the bear when it came within eight feet of him. The bear approached closer; rather than stand his ground, Jeremy fled.

Though it was mid-September and the lake water was chilly, Jeremy sprinted toward the lake, made his way down the rocky embankment, and dove. A strong swimmer, he made his way fifty feet out into the lake before deciding to yell back to James to warn him of the bear. He turned toward shore and found himself face to face with a swimming bear.

In nearly the same instant that Jeremy tried to get away, the bear bit into the front of his left thigh. When Jeremy pushed at the bear's head, the attacker grabbed his wrist and then his shoulder. When Jeremy turned to try and get away, the bear let go of his shoulder and grabbed him by the back of the neck.

By this time, James had made his way to the lake's edge. Seeing his father helpless, he yelled, cursed frantically, and charged out into the water. Fueled by a charge of adrenaline, James managed to drag both the bear and his father into shallow water. The bear maintained its grip on Jeremy's neck and tried shaking the two-hundred-pound man. James was on top of the bear and his father, and both men were trying to loosen the bear's vicelike grip.

"I absolutely felt, at that point," Jeremy recollects, "that I was going to die." Frantic, James yelled, "What do I do, what do I do!" With an amazing calmness, Jeremy told his son to get something to hit the bear with. Jamie ran up the bank, grabbed a canoe paddle, returned to the bear, and started hitting it in the face. Afraid that he might accidentally strike his father, James positioned himself behind the bear and struck the bear in back of the skull. Luck-

Above: When camping in canoe country, some campers prefer to camp on islands to lessen the chance of a confrontation with a bear. However, bears are very good swimmers, and some bears have been known to swim over half a mile in order to check out a campsite. (Photo copyright by Jeanne Drake)

Overleaf: While mother and cub take a break from the usual foraging, they hardly appear as the image of "ferocious bears." (Photo copyright by James H. Robinson)

Of the North American bears, the black is perhaps the most adaptable to human encroachment. But it has its own threshold of tolerance, and eventually it too must move on to more remote habitat—habitat that is diminishing. As more and more wild land is being claimed by commercial and economic interests, the black bears' range will shrink. (Photo copyright by Michael H. Francis)

ily, when the paddle broke, the bear finally released its grip and ran up the bank.

Jeremy staggered over to the loaded canoe and collapsed into it, while James grabbed another paddle and jumped into the stern. As he backpaddled from shore, the men looked back and were horrified to see the bear swimming back out toward them. However, with the advantage of the canoe and a surge of adrenalin, James soon outdistanced the bear.

With the help of another party of canoeists, an Indian fishing guide, a float plane at a fly-in camp, and a seventy-five-mile ambulance ride, Jeremy was finally delivered to a hospital—eight hours after the attack. At the hospital he was treated for nineteen puncture wounds.

Oddly enough, on the morning of the same day that Jeremy was attacked, the float plane had flown a similar mercy mission—a bear-attack victim from the same lake. The victim, a young man on his solo experience of an Outward Bound adventure, had been attacked. Besides puncture wounds, he experienced a broken collarbone when the bear attempted to drag him off into the woods. His screams had been heard across the water by nearby Outward Bounders. Only after they dealt canoe-paddle blows to the bear did it retreat.

Recognizing that a real problem bear was threatening campers, a team of state personnel flew into the lake and found a bear terrorizing another campsite on an island several miles from the site of the Cleaveland attack. The bear was killed, and after examination of its stomach contents, it was determined that the same bear was involved in each of the three attacks.

The bear, a six- to eight-year-old female, was very thin and weighed only 117 pounds. Considering it was well into fall, it is unlikely that this bear would have accumulated enough fat to survive the winter. Natural food production was very poor in the area of the bear's attacks in 1987 and might have been the reason for the attacks.

A MEETING WITH THE BEARS

Most Americans and Canadians will never see a black bear in the wild. Period. Yet that very prospect is terrifying to most folks.

More people are killed by pet dog attacks, horse-riding accidents, and farm accidents involving cattle every year than the grand total of folks who have died from black bear attacks since 1900—fewer than thirty. The larger, more aggressive grizzly bear has been involved in more fatal human encounters than has the black bear. And it is even less likely that Americans and Canadians will ever encounter a grizzly bear because the grizzlies' numbers are far fewer than the black bears', and their home range is generally in remote back country.

"It's safer sleeping naked in woods filled with black bears than

The greatest threat to the black bear in the western part of its range is our society's demand for more timber. Excessive logging, particularly in the national forests, could cause declines in localized populations of bears. This brown-phased black bear has the best chance of survival if its habitat remains intact. (Photo copyright by Michael H. Francis)

driving sixty-five miles per hour on a U.S. interstate highway!" says canoe country guide Cliff Jacobson. "My advice," Jacobson adds, "is to walk unafraid into the wilderness, but treat every bear you meet with respect."

These sentiments are shared by wildlife biologist Karen Noyce, who has been working with northern Minnesota black bears in a Department of Natural Resources ten-year-long study. Noyce herself has crawled into over three hundred of the five-hundred-plus bear dens that have been investigated during the winter. During the summer months, many bears have been captured in large culvert traps or in snares and are generally more aggressive than the lethargic denned bears. Yet Noyce has never had what she considers a "close call" with a bear—and neither have any of her fellow biologists. Noyce shared, "The worst thing we have ever had happen was when a person who accompanied us to a den fell on a stick and had to have some serious surgery on an eye. The accident had nothing to do with the bear itself."

Like most people, I grew up hearing that you should never be in the vicinity of a mother bear and her cubs or yearlings. Such a confrontation, I was led to believe, would probably result in a bear attack and likely my death. Yet, of the black bear biologists that I've talked to, none of them has been attacked by a mother bear. Noyce explains that in the first weeks of the study project, they carried a rifle in the truck for protection, but after their first few encounters with females and cubs in which they drugged the cubs to gather blood samples and data, they left the gun behind. The firearm has never accompanied the biologists since.

Lynn Rogers, known to many as the "Bearman," has studied black bears in Michigan and Minnesota for over twenty-three years, and he has handled hundreds of bears. He insists that there should "not be a cause for great concern in finding yourself between cubs and the mother." However, it is important to note that there have been records of human injuries—not deaths— when a mother bear was apparently defending her cubs from an overly curious or careless human. Any occasion a person comes near a mother black bear and cubs should be treated as potentially dangerous, even though the incidence of attack is rare.

"Even with cubs," Rogers assures, "black bears usually retreat." Just as a brooding female ruffed grouse might fan her tail, raise her neck ruff feathers, and aggressively come toward you hissing and mewing, she is not going to take you on. She sees you as a potential threat to her brood of chicks and does her best to intimidate you. Noyce explains, "Even with cubs in a culvert trap and the mother free outside, a seemingly threatening situation, we have never had any trouble from the mother. She might make a lot of noise in the surrounding brush and huff some, but that is the extent of her actions."

Canadian wildlife biologist Stephen Herrero contrasts the

grizzly and black bear mothers in *Bear Attacks:* "The grizzly bear mother shows a more aggressive protection of offspring." Herrero explains that, unlike the forest-dwelling black bear, the grizzly bear evolved in an open, treeless environment, a tundra landscape at the edge of the retreating glaciers. The grizzlies' long claws were perfect tools for digging plant foods such as roots and bulbs, but they were not well suited for tree climbing. Consequently, faced with a potential threat, the grizzly cubs cannot or do not climb into the safety of a tree. Instead, the mother has no choice but to aggressively defend her young. Herrero believes that, in areas where humans and black bears coexist on a regular basis, most bear attack injuries result from bears trying to get at people's food or from humans not giving bears enough space. In such a situation, Herrero feels it is best to give up your food if a bear is persistent rather than risk an unnecessary injury. Moving away from the bear should make the bear feel less threatened by your presence.

Herrero believes that statistically speaking, those bears that become conditioned to human foods offer the greatest danger to humans. There is also the rare occasion, particularly when the bear's natural foods are in short supply, that a black bear assumes the role of a predator and views humans as prey.

So what should you do if a bear does attack? A couple of years after Jeremy Cleaveland was attacked by a black bear, he asked biologist Lynn Rogers for advice if he were ever attacked again. Rogers explained to Cleaveland that another attack was highly unlikely, but if confronted again, he should act aggressively toward the bear and not run from it. Such advice concurs with Herrero's findings, as noted in *Bear Attacks:* When a black bear assumes a predatory notion, ". . . a person should use every inner resource and available weapon (even if it is only your foot or fist) to try to fight off the bear. . . . People who run away or people who act passively or play dead are simply inviting the bear to continue the attack." Repellents, similar to those used by walking postal carriers to fend off aggressive dogs, have been found to be very effective against bears. Those repellents containing capsaicin, an active ingredient of cayenne peppers, appear to ward off a "too close" bear the best. The repellent is under pressure and is sprayed into the bear's face, and testing has found no permanent damage to animals' eyes. Such repellents are available through sporting goods stores and catalogs.

When asked if he would return to the canoe country to camp where his attack occurred, Cleaveland answered, "I really believe that this was an extremely rare situation, and the likelihood of an attack happening to me was probably a million to one, and for it to repeat itself is even more remote." Only four autumns after the attack, Jeremy is planning to paddle with his youngest son into

Just as black bears scavenge on other animals' kills, they don't hesitate to feed on human garbage. Sights such as this are common in many parts of the black bear's range. (Photo copyright by John & Ann Mahan)

the same canoe country he visited with attack survivor and son James.

It is difficult to know whether a bear is simply curious or whether it is a threat. Recognizing the difference is a matter of interpreting the bear's behavior, and it is not easy to distinguish between a naturally curious, human-food-conditioned, or a predaceous bear in a few minutes' span, let alone in seconds. The best rule to follow is, in all confrontations with a lone bear or a sow and her cubs—even if they don't seem threatening, treat the situation as *potentially* dangerous. If the bear appears persistent and you notice that its ears are flattened on a lowered head, or that it is walking in a stiff-legged stalk or crouched in a waiting posture, it is best to stop what you are doing and slowly back away. If the bear still acts belligerently and aggressively, you need to act as aggressively as you can: Yell and throw stones or sticks. If there are several people in your group, do not surround the bear; give it an avenue of escape. A "herd" of people will be more impressive and dominating to the bear.

WINTERING WITH
A BLACK BEAR

"There is a sense of expectancy, a waiting and a breathlessness. The rustling sounds are gone, the scurryings and small, dry movements of fall. There is a hush, a deep and quiet breathing after the hurried and colored violence of the months just gone. Suddenly the air is white with drifting flakes. . . ." Sigurd Olson, *The Singing Wilderness*

It was only seven days until the spring equinox, when the sun would finally give us more daylight than darkness. Yet under our snowshoes was two to three feet of snow. The energy of a coming spring was not evident, even though the sun illuminated the maze of stark, leafless birches that lay before us. From the screen of birches off to our left came the slow, methodical, heavy probes of a pileated woodpecker as it sculpted its way into the winter gallery for a meal of treebound carpenter ants. Somewhere out ahead of us, in the vast Chippewa National Forest north of Grand Rapids, Minnesota, there was a bear. We were not following its trail; instead we followed the beckoning *chirp* of a radio transmitter that was built into a hefty collar encircling the neck of a hibernating bear.

This was not just any bear. This one had an identity: #78, a ten-year-old female who was fitted with her first radio collar as a yearling in 1982. She and her two littermates were fondly known among the Department of Natural Resources researchers as the "three sisters." Both sisters had died, and #78 had the honor of wearing a radio collar longer than any other bear in the ten-year black bear study project.

Quietly the four of us, three state-employed researchers and me, shuffled single-file down the slope toward a meeting with bears. Suddenly Pam Coy, a wildlife technician who was leading

For the black bear, winter does not begin at the winter solstice, but usually in mid-fall. By this time, it should be well fattened as food sources are becoming scarce. The bear's final acts before winter are to search for a suitable denning site and then to pull together materials for a nest. (Photo copyright by Tom Walker)

the way with her headphones hooked up to the radio receiver, paused and held up her hand in a signal for us to stop. Alone, she made her way to a pair of large, downed aspen trees. The intertwined roots of the two trees had pulled partially out of the ground, giving rise to a large snow-covered mound. Unseen beneath the mound was #78 and her three yearling cubs. In the quiet language of hand signals and familiarity with a job, the three researchers, Pam, Bobbie Allen (an intern helping on the bear project), and Karen Noyce began gathering the data.

Noyce is a veteran bear-den visitor, and in short order, clad in her work coveralls and a homemade woven stocking hat, she was wriggling through the den opening. She held a four-foot-long aspen shoot. Taped on the shoot's end was a hypodermic syringe, which held a dose of a mixture of anesthesia and muscle relaxant. Several minutes passed. There was no blood-curdling growl, although Noyce later confided that the mother bear "did huff a bit" when the bear felt the prick of the needle.

With our help, Noyce carefully hauled the drugged adult bear from the winter den. Within fifteen minutes, #78's three yearlings, two females and a male, were carefully pulled out and placed on unrolled foam pads to await processing.

While I slowly ran my bared hands through the adult bear's luxurious, glistening black coat, the DNR trio began their coordinated task of getting as much data as they could from the bears. They collected blood and hair samples from each animal for testing back at the lab in Grand Rapids. They measured the animals' body lengths, paws, teeth, leg bones, chest girth, tails, and skulls. The researchers took each bear's temperature and weight and checked pulse and respiration rates. The adult weighed 181 pounds, down from 194 a year previous. Karen surmised that the mother had put on less fat because she was nursing cubs throughout most of the previous summer, causing an energy drain on herself.

While the data-gathering was going on, Pam casually noted that the adult bear was starting to come around. The bear was given a booster shot of the anesthesia to prolong her sleep a bit longer. Because I wasn't of much help, I walked over to the den, crawled in, and wondered. Some claim extremes build character. If that is the case, then winter is an unequalled sculptor of character.

Most life copes with winter either by risking the dangers of migration and avoiding winter or by adapting to the snow and cold. Snow, the very definition of winter in the black bear's northern range, provides tremendous heat-trapping insulation because there are millions of air pockets between the loosely tumbled snowflakes. The ruffed grouse is content to winter in the northern woods, particularly if there is a thick blanket of soft, fluffy snow under which it can roost during the coldest nights.

Bear researchers such as Pam Coy of the Minnesota Department of Natural Resources are able to locate denning bears with the help of radio-tracking equipment. The study animal wears a neck collar that has a transmitter affixed to it. The transmitter gives off a pulsing chirp that grows in intensity as the researcher moves closer. During the summer months, the researchers can track a bear's movements and rate of travel or determine the habitat that the bear frequents. (Photo copyright by Tom Anderson)

Left: After the hibernating adult bear is sedated, a rope is carefully harnessed over the limp bear to aid in pulling the bear from its den. Minnesota Department of Natural Resources biologist Karen Noyce (at the den entrance) and project intern Bobbie Allen prepare to pull an adult female bear from her den in order to gather information. (Photo copyright by Tom Anderson)

Above right: This yearling bear has just been fitted with a radio collar. Through the course of its life, the bear will be followed and occasionally found and sedated to adjust the collar, replace a worn-out radio, and monitor the bear's physiological changes. The researchers use extreme care to insure the bear's well-being, and within an hour or so, this bear was shrugging off the effects of the sedative. (Photo copyright by Tom Anderson)

Below right: Bear researcher Karen Noyce is using a calipers to measure the bear's canine teeth. Each bear undergoes a multitude of measurements, such as weight, girth, and length. The data is gathered, fed into a computer program, and analyzed. Such information provides insight to the growth and health of the individual bear and the overall population. (Photo copyright by Tom Anderson)

The moose face winter as well, and they meander through the thick willow and dogwood thickets and wade through the deep snow on stilt-legs. Their shorter-legged cousins, the whitetail deer, have more of a problem traveling through snow, but they follow the trodden winter trails where the snow has been packed down by other deer. The deer appear more social at this time of the year because they often congregate (yard-up) in areas that offer both protection from the heat-robbing winds and nourishment found by browsing on some of the shrubs. The groups of deer keep the snow packed down and offer more eyes and ears to detect any approaching threat. On the other hand, the warblers, thrushes, and vireos that had nested here in these woods a few months ago winter in the southerly tropics, where the bite of cold is nonexistent and their needed fuel of insects and fruits is plentiful.

Like a bear, a woodchuck (or groundhog) accumulates fat over the summer and fall, and it retreats to a prepared den for the winter. But unlike a bear, a woodchuck's metabolic functions come practically to a standstill: Its heart and respiration rates drop down to less than a dozen beats and breaths per minute, and its body temperature falls from a normal summer high of approximately 104 degrees Fahrenheit to a chilly 37 to 39 degrees. Such a "sleep" has always been considered the definition of hibernation and is what small, winter-dormant mammals usually experience.

The black bear, lacking wings or limbs for efficient long-distance travel, is a marvel at winter adaptation. According to bear biologist Lynn Rogers, bears are "extra-sophisticated hibernators." Even though the bear's den is usually only slightly warmer than the air outside, a black bear's winter body temperature, generally 93 to 94 degrees Fahrenheit, does not significantly drop from its summer temperature range of 102 to 106 degrees. To maintain such a high body temperature, a bear must burn calories—up to four thousand per day. At such a rate, the bear will lose weight, and over the winter most adult bears lost 15 to 25 percent of their prehibernation weight. Unlike the more torpid woodchuck, the bear is able to arouse itself fairly quickly while hibernating because of this higher winter body temperature. Such a strategy might help it react to danger more quickly than most other hibernators.

For roughly five months (or the time that the bear is hibernating), from November through March, most bears in the northern United States and southern Canada will not eat, drink, nor even defecate. Such a feat indeed makes this animal a sophisticated hibernator. To pull this off, black bears recycle their metabolic wastes. Ralph Nelson, director of medicine at the University of Illinois College of Medicine, has studied the complex processes for nearly twenty years. Nelson has discovered that during hibernation the bear produces energy by burning its fat reserves rather

Above: We tend to believe that bears hibernate in caves. Most choose an underground den or a den beneath the tangled limbs of a fallen tree. However, some bears, such as this one, choose to create an open nest. Where the climate is cold enough, winter will insulate the bears with a blanket of snow. (Photo copyright by Dave Garshelis, Minnesota Department of Natural Resources)

Below: Just as humans curl into a ball when chilled, a bear assumes the same fetal position in the winter den to lessen exposure to its thinner-furred underbelly. The bear also pulls its four limbs into the ball to reduce further exposure. Such tactics are important energy-conserving practices. (Photo copyright by Dave Garshelis, Minnesota Department of Natural Resources)

than protein (as a human does). By burning only fat in its metabolic furnace, the bear reduces the buildup of urea (nitrogen-containing wastes in the blood that would have been produced had the bear burned protein). The bear also meets its need for water because the byproducts of metabolized fat are water and carbon dioxide. In the end, the water and carbon dioxide are disposed of as the hibernating bear exhales, whatever urea exists breaks down, and the nitrogen is recycled into protein.

How do bears remain inactive for such a long period without experiencing any bone weakening or loss? If the bones break down and dump extra calcium into the blood system, dangerous levels of calcium could be fatal to the animal. Nelson has also found that somehow, black bears are able to recycle calcium and actually generate bone over the winter. Findings indicate that bone-building takes place in different places within the bear's body in the winter than in the summer. The process is most likely concentrated in those areas that are bearing the weight of the prostrate bear. Nelson and other researchers believe that black bears have many secrets that might prove valuable in the future treatment of human kidney disease or bone diseases such as osteoporosis.

Perhaps most amazing is that black bears give birth in the latter part of January or early February, usually to two or three cubs. No other terrestrial mammal in North America gives birth so early in the year. Being mammals, the young must be nourished by their mother's milk, which is another drain on mother's fat stores. Pregnant females do not necessarily store more fat than nonpregnant females or males. If a pregnant female enters hibernation with inadequate fat supplies, her young, either unborn or born, will suffer and have a lesser chance of survival.

At birth, the cubs weigh one-half to three-quarters of a pound and are hairless. Though the mother is still hibernating, she is alert to the birth process and will lick the cubs clean as each is born. The newborn cubs must have warmth and nourishment, which the mother provides. The mother bear's body heat and her warm breath provide the needed heat for the cubs. Curled in a fetal position, nose-to-tail, the cubs, safely tucked in a snug pocket, find the mother bear's nipples. Researcher Noyce explains that the mother supports some of her weight on her front torso and legs so that the cubs actually spend much of their time underneath their mother. If the mother bear relaxes or shifts so that some of her weight bears down on a cub, the cub's squeal will signal the mother to reshift herself until all is quiet among her youngsters. The cubs are well nourished by their mother's milk, which is approximately 25 percent fat; for comparison, human milk is less than 4 percent fat. In the den, the sluggish mother will lick the cubs, stimulating them to defecate. The mother then consumes the cubs' waste. In so doing, she recycles nutrients that

This brown-colored black bear cub receives security and warmth from its mother. Sharing body heat (call it cuddling if you like) is an efficient means of coping with frigid temperatures. This adult bear is sedated as she awaits inspection by the bear biologists. It is not necessary to sedate the young cubs during a data-gathering excursion. (Photo copyright by Pam Coy, Minnesota Department of Natural Resources)

have passed through the cubs' digestive system. This also keeps the den clean, lessening the chance of predators such as timber wolves detecting the den by smelling the cache of denned bears. Noyce has occasionally seen tracks of wolves that have approached the entrance of a den, stopped—perhaps to assess the situation, and then moved on. (There have been cases where wolves have killed bears in a winter den.) In a matter of two to three months, when the cubs crawl out into a world of early spring, they will have grown coats of fur and increased in weight by sixteen-fold to approximately eight pounds.

As I reflected on the bears' past few months, I was amazed at how four bears could all fit in the cozy space I now occupied. In the main chamber was the nesting material that the mother had raked in with her claws during the previous October. Most of the nest was made up of dried grasses, leaves, and mosses. There was no bear scat, no overwhelming bear odor, just the smells of leaves and earth. I crawled out of the bears' winter dwelling and rejoined the DNR team.

As Coy fitted one of the yearlings with its first radio collar, she said, "I dub you #5381." The number referred to the radio frequency that the transmitter was set at. From then on, the cub's location could be determined just by switching the receiver to its frequency. Most of the study bears' seasonal locations were monitored by the biologists, who passed overhead in weekly aircraft flights.

Two hours had passed since Noyce had first crawled into den #294, and she was back into the den, trying her best to arrange four very relaxed bears into some semblance of comfort. The rest of us were packing equipment into the backpack when we heard the muffled yells of a semidenned Noyce. In her contortions of trying to get the last yearling into place, she had gotten stuck. Her muffled yells were deciphered, and I grabbed her flailing boots and pulled. Out she came, face muddied, her thick, single brown braid a bit tattered, but wearing a grin that seemed to say, "All in a day's work." In minutes, we snowshoed up through the slope of birch and left winter and a sloth of bears behind us.

Some bears hibernate before the first snowfall, and others continue searching for food late into the fall. This bear is stripping off a section of aspen bark in hopes of finding dormant insects or a surprised mouse that might add to the bear's collection of fat. (Photo copyright by Tom Walker)

WHAT'S AHEAD FOR THE BLACK BEAR?

Though the population numbers fall short of historical highs before human intervention, only two of the eight bear species in the world, the polar bear and the black bear, are experiencing overall increases in their numbers (although this increase is not occurring across all of the black bear's habitat). Both species are responding to management practices humans impose. Does this suggest that the future of all bears lies at the hands of humans and how we perceive these great mammals?

Obviously, the earth is no smaller than it was 25 million years ago when the first bears evolved. But what has shrunk is the habitat these animals need to survive. As the human population continues to climb, there is a corresponding increase in the demand for agricultural areas to raise food for the burgeoning mass of humans. Such lands are often found in black bear haunts. And, the demand for natural resources grows. With more people come more homes, and more homes mean more lumber. Ultimately there is a reduction of mature forest of the sort that black bears prefer. Already some of the black bear populations in the western states are experiencing declines due to the loss of habitat, poaching, and killing of "nuisance" bears.

Problems will continue for the black bear as long as humans remain careless and ignorant with the disposal of garbage and storage of food in black bear country. Young black bears raised at a dump or dependent on the food of careless campers have no future. The answer lies in a better educated public that understands the connection of black bears to the environment.

Fragmentation has become somewhat of a buzzword in the past few years in light of what is happening to both the tropical rainforests and the northern forests. Maintaining prime bear habitat remains a key issue if the black bear is to remain a dweller of

The future of the black bear depends on the quality of the habitat. As humans encroach into wild areas where vast, mature forests remain, the bears will be pushed into smaller forest fragments. Our seemingly insatiable appetite for more and more of the earth's resources will likely threaten not only bears, but also countless other forms of life. (Photo copyright by Tom Walker)

the North American forests. Much attention has been given to the plight of our songbirds, such as the thrushes, warblers, and tanagers, as the forests become forest pieces. But the black bear is also pushed into shrinking forests and out into marginal habitat, where the bear is more likely to encounter humans. New roads are built into these wild areas and, consequently, the incidence of road-killed bears rises. If pressed to find the needed food to accumulate its winter fat, the bear is often forced to resort to human crops, trash, and picnic baskets.

In recent years, the black bear has been designated as a game animal in most states and provinces. Each state or province regulates the hunt and establishes the dates and times that the bear can be hunted by a bear license holder. Regulation has been good news for overall black bear numbers. No longer is it legal to indiscriminately kill a black bear during any time or day of the year, unless one's life is threatened. Many states have all-time-high bear numbers even with annual bear-hunting seasons. For example, in Minnesota it is estimated that well over ten thousand, and perhaps more than fifteen thousand, bears roam the state. In 1990 a record kill of 2,350 bears were tagged, and another record harvest is predicted for 1991. Minnesota bear populations are monitored on a regional basis, and the harvests are consequently controlled by adjusting the number of hunters in each region to achieve desired bear populations.

Another problem looms on the horizon for the black bear, and it is of international scope. Bear body parts, particularly the gall bladder, are believed to have medicinal value. The Asian bears are in particular danger of being completely reduced to the level that their populations may not recover. Black bears are not immune to the body part market. The primary market for bear parts, including black bear parts, is in Asia. But because the source for black bear parts is North American, bear poaching is on the rise across the continent. So far, undercover operations have nabbed more than one hundred poachers and dealers in bear body parts. With bear galls fetching retail prices of $400 to $600 apiece on the West Coast of the United States, it is not surprising that the illegal trade is on the rise. The startling decrease of African elephants for want of ivory is proof enough of what human greed can do to an animal species.

Some people will never change their opinion of the black bear; to them it will always be a "big, bad bear." Somewhere beneath the frightening stereotypes of that bad bear lies a gentle creature that in fact is a genetic spin-off of the wolf and "man's best friend," the dog. Just as our canine companions become dependent on humans for their well-being and survival, the bear's future depends on human attitudes rather than a daily dose of love and food.

To add to our fears, we are likely to read of more and more

The innumerable questions that researchers ask about what makes a black bear function will be answered with continuing research. Improved data and logical interpretation of findings will benefit the black bear. (Note this bear's tagged ear.) (Photo copyright by Bill Lea)

bear attacks on humans in the coming years. With a greater number of people seeking outdoor experiences in a limited offering of remote settings, more folks are likely to encounter black bears. Humans and bears will cross paths more often, and, with an increase in interactions, it is likely that more injuries, to both bears and humans, will result. There will likely be more cases where livestock owners and honey producers will have more encounters with bears threatening their livelihood. When newsworthy conflicts with bears occur there will likely be a loud demand that the "nuisance" bears be removed. It is time that we realize we are the "nuisance."

In truth, when we point to most environmental problems we can conclude that the problems are of human origin. Not only do we demand more natural resources than any other species on earth, but it seems that we have forgotten that we are but a piece of the whole spectrum of diverse life forms on this planet, just as the bear is. The bear would fare better if we served as steward rather than master.

Humans are fond of symbols, and the black bear is a worthy symbol of the forest. Bear biologist Steve Herrero reverently claims that the black bear is the "spirit of the forest." We cannot afford to lose such symbols. Only by unlocking the secrets of the black bear's life and by erasing some of the deep-set biases that many people have about bears can we come to respect, appreciate, and secure the future of the black bear.

I asked bear researcher Karen Noyce if she had ever experienced nightmares inspired from her hundreds of visits to active bear dens. She couldn't recall any horrible dreams, but she did share a strange one.

"In the dream, I was horrified to find that the male bear we been radio-tracking had had its collar slip down from its neck to its waist. I felt awful about the bear's discomfort, and wondered if all this data-gathering to find out about the bear's movements and what they eat was really necessary. As I worked on the bear to reposition the collar back to the neck, the bear suddenly spoke slowly and clearly to me. It asked, "Why don't you just ask what you want to know?"

And so perhaps our dialogue with the bears should include, "Teach us respect, teach us to share, and teach us to be your true voice."

We need a human population informed of the importance of the black bear's role if the bear is to remain on earth. Stereotypes will have to be erased. From its vantage point, the bear sees that its future is dependent on human action. (Photo copyright by Michael H. Francis)

Saving Space for the Black Bear

Amid the battle between economic expansion and the necessity of wilderness, work to study and conserve the haunts of the black bear pushes on in essential pockets all across North America. Interested readers may find more information from these organizations, or from state or provincial departments of wildlife.

For those interested in all aspects of bears, bear biology, and bear habitat, contact the North American Bear Society at 9601 North 120th Street, Scottsdale, Arizona 85259. Members of the society receive *Ursus*, a quarterly, full-color magazine.

Along the rugged coast of British Columbia, wildlife biologists with the Valhalla Wilderness Society pursue the extremely rare, little-studied Kermode, a subspecies of the black bear that occurs only in British Columbia's majestic coastal rain forest. Among the Kermode's population are a few all-white individuals that have sparked names such as "ghost," "snow," and "spirit" bears. One of the goals of the society: the establishment of the Spirit Bear Park Reserve on Princess Royal Island in Canada. For more information, write the Valhalla Wilderness Society, Box 224, New Denver, British Columbia, V0G 1S0.

We would do well to learn from many Native Americans' perspective of the bear. To them, the bear was a most spiritually powerful animal and commanded great respect. Today, it should be as sincerely regarded. (Photo copyright by Bill Lea)

REFERENCES

Cahalane, Victor H. *Mammals of North America.* New York: The Macmillan Company, 1947.

Cleaveland, Jeremy. Telephone interview with the author. Spring 1991.

Dewey, Donald. *Bears.* New York: Friedman Publishing Group, Inc., 1991.

Ford, Barbara. *Black Bear, The Spirit of the Wilderness.* Boston: Houghton Mifflin Company, 1981.

Herrero, Stephen. *Bear Attacks: Their Causes and Avoidance.* Piscataway, NJ: Winchester Press, 1985.

_____. Lecture at the Science Museum of Minnesota, St. Paul, MN, 1990.

Kayser, Richard. Interview with author. Spring 1991.

McCrory, Wayne. Letters to editor. Winter 1991 and spring 1992.

_____, and Bart Robinson. "A Proposal for a 'Spirit Bear Class A Marine-Provincial Park Reserve' on Southern Princess Royal Island." Brief to Parks and Wilderness 90s, April 1991.

McLaughlin, Craig R. Letter to editor. Winter 1991.

McLoughlin, John C. *The Canine Clan: A New Look at Man's Best Friend.* New York: The Viking Press, 1983.

Nelson, Richard K. *Make Prayers to the Raven.* Chicago: University of Chicago Press, 1986.

Noyce, Karen. Letter to editor. Winter 1991.

Nordberg, Ken. *Do-It-Yourself Black Bear Baiting and Hunting.* Minneapolis, MN: Shingle Creek Outdoor Productions, 1990.

Pringle, Laurence. *Bearman: Exploring the World of Black Bears.* New York: Charles Scribner's Sons, 1989.

Revkin, Andrew C. "Sleeping Beauties." *Discover,* April 1989, 62–65.

Rogers, Lynn. "A Bear in its Lair." *Natural History,* October 1981, 64–70.

_____. *How to Live with Black Bears.* St. Paul, MN: North Central Forest Experiment Station, U.S. Forest Service, 1988.

_____. Lecture at the Science Museum of Minnesota, 1990.

Stokes, Donald and Lillian Stokes. *A Guide to Animal Tracking and Behavior.* Boston-Toronto: Little, Brown and Company, 1987.

Van Wormer, Joe. *The World of the Black Bear.* Philadelphia and New York: J.B. Lippincott Company, 1966.

Wickelgren, Ingrid. "Bone Loss and the Three Bears." *Science News,* Dec. 24 & 31, 1988, 424–425.

Wright, William H. *The Black Bear.* New York: Charles Scribner's Sons, 1910.

(Photo copyright by Tom Walker)

"The Uninvited Guest" by painter Philip R. Goodwin depicts a not-too-rare occurence in canoe country.

INDEX

ABOUT THE AUTHOR

After graduating with a degree in wildlife biology from the University of Minnesota, Tom Anderson worked with the Department of Natural Resources and as a director for the Chisago County Parks Department. Since 1977, he has worked as a teacher and naturalist for the Lee and Rose Warner Nature Center in Marine-on-St. Croix, Minnesota. He currently is director of the center, which is operated by the Science Museum of Minnesota.

Anderson is the author of *Learning Nature by a Country Road*, published by Voyageur Press in 1989, and is a contributing writer to *North Writers: A Strong Woods Collection*, published by the University of Minnesota Press. His work is frequently published in *St. Croix Magazine* and *Minnesota Sportsman*. For ten years, he wrote an award-winning weekly column, "Reading Sign," for the *Chisago County Press*.

Overleaf: (Photo copyright by Bill Lea)